CONSCIOUSNESS
AND
ENERGY
VOLUME 4

TRUMP, THE STING, THE CATASTROPHE CYCLE AND CONSCIOUSNESS

PENNY KELLY

CONSCIOUSNESS AND ENERGY, VOL. 4
TRUMP, THE STING,
THE CATASTROPHE CYCLE
AND CONSCIOUSNESS

BY

PENNY KELLY

Published by:
Lily Hill Publishing
32260 – 88th Avenue
Lawton, MI 49065
www.pennykelly.com

ISBN: 978-09632934-9-7

Book and Cover Design by Penny Kelly
Front Cover Photo: Eta Carinae Nebula
NASA/JPL Spitzer Space Telescope 2016
This false-color image taken by NASA's Spitzer Space Telescope shows the "South Pillar" region of the star-forming region called the Carina Nebula. Like cracking open a watermelon and finding its seeds, the infrared telescope "busted open" this murky cloud to reveal star embryos (yellow or white) tucked inside finger-like pillars of thick dust (pink). Though the nebula's most famous and massive star, Eta Carinae, is too bright to be observed by infrared telescopes, the downward-streaming rays hint at its presence above the picture frame. Ultraviolet radiation and stellar winds from Eta Carinae and its siblings have shredded the cloud to pieces, leaving a mess of tendrils and pillars. This shredding process triggered the birth of the new stars uncovered by Spitzer.

Dedication

*This book is dedicated to those
who have been afraid
for reasons they cannot explain,
and to all who hold even the tiniest
spark of love for other
humans, plants, animals,
stars, planets, experiences, and places
both sacred and profane,
even the things we have built or manufactured,
for whether or not
that spark of love is
admitted, justified, legal,
sensible, expressed, or recognized...
it is still love
and the tiniest spark makes
a world
of difference.*

Table of Contents

Introduction

THIS BOOK STARTED OUT AS AN ESSAY TITLED *TRUMP AND THE STING*. I wrote it because I was trying to sort out, organize, and make sense of what I saw going on in the world around me. Once it was finished, I shared it with a few people. They liked it so I added it to my website as an e-book, thinking that maybe it would help a few other people get a grip on what was going on in our country. To my surprise, it became an instant best-seller on my site and sold more than my full-length books!

After reading it, some wrote to say they could not stand Donald Trump and weren't going to start liking him no matter what I wrote. I would read such comments and shake my head. My goal was not to make people love Trump. It was to help them understand what was going on in our government and our country so they can see past Trump to our future.

Not long after the essay began selling, people began writing to ask for a sequel, an update, or anything else that might help them keep abreast of what was going on behind the curtain of public events. They were interested in the hidden moves being made. This is that sequel. It is more than the original essay and covers some of what is going on in the U.S., information about the sun's micro-nova process, and the need to develop consciousness in order to successfully deal with all of this.

The book looks first at the group I call the Cabal and their plan to take over the world. Then we examine information that has been hidden for decades regarding the sun and the micro-nova that occurs every 12,068 years. From there we go on to look at the development of consciousness and how this can be used to prepare for the changes in both our country and our solar system.

Many people and groups have wanted to control the world and be at the top of the power pile. I think it's time for us, the ordinary people who are not so ordinary after all, to expand consciousness to the point that we take responsbility for creating the world we want to live in. It's time to come down from the power pile we have been climbing and spread out in a circle that holds all life as worthwhile and needed. Each of us is unique, and that is the gift we bring to the circle.

As you read, keep in mind something that many people seem to have forgotten: there is a big difference between government and Hollywood. Politicians are supposed to be working for us, thoughtfully producing laws that protect our rights. Their job is to preserve the republic in which we live. Actors are in the business of creating illusions. Their job is to entertain us for a while. It's a bonus if the entertainment is educational, but education is no substitute for government. There is a subtle difference between education and propaganda, and a glaring difference between a government and Hollywood—or at least there should be.

If we lose our republic, we will be stuck with only a democracy. Democracy is nothing more than *majority rule*, which, in the end, almost always translates to *mob rule*. Whoever has the most power dictates the rules and there are no checks and balances to protect the rights of the human being. The rights of a human being are god-given and take precedence over any system of laws and governments, and therein is the difference between a republic and a democracy. A republic recognizes and protects those god-given rights, whereas a democracy dictates what rights you will be allowed to have.[1] Hollywood may create movies that celebrate

---

1 Still, Bill. *"A Democracy or a Republic?"* Still Report #2642, 7 June 2019. https://www.youtube.com/watch?v=RpdtFO9ASXs&t=435s/.

democracy, but if we forget that what we have is a republic, we will have lost an irreplaceable treasure.

People often want to immigrate to America because they want to live in a system that recognizes and honors their god-given rights to life, freedom, and permission to become the best they can be. They want to develop themselves without interference unless they are doing something harmful to others. We may think people want to come here for money or access to material things, and those are big attractors, but the real draws are the rights, the freedoms, the permissions, and the recognition of the human regardless of class or station in life. Money and material things arise from those rights, freedoms, and permissions.

At times, people write to me and ask, "Why do you write about politics or finance? Why don't you just stick to spirituality and consciousness?" This is silo thinking. Consciousness creates everything in reality, and true spirituality is the spirit with which a person, business, or institution conducts itself. When I write about politics and finance, I *am* writing about spirituality and consciousness! The spirit with which you conduct your consciousness is the spirituality embedded in everyday reality. Thus, spirituality is not limited to churches or religion; it is embedded in everything from politics, finance, and food to relationships, education, healing, and beyond. People are so used to narrow perceptions and the imaginary rules of politically-correct thinking that they are not able to apply spirituality to everyday living.

The spirit of a reality system will determine whether it lives or dies, so I will continue to write about the things going on in our reality, including the politics. I do so because *government is a reflection of consciousness* and a very clear symbol of how we are managing ourselves and our relationships with others around the planet.

In writing the original essay, I skipped over many historical facts that I thought were understood by the general population. I am not trying to explain the intricate details that would be required in a historical tract, I am trying to pull the curtain back on what goes on behind the scenes and to flesh things out a little more for those who do not have time to dig into what is going on.

Keep in mind that I try to write from the perspective of the forces in consciousness that are at play in our lives and the results in our reality. This does not negate the facts, it's just that facts are too often used as an excuse to argue. There are many things that we agree on when it comes to reports about *what* happened in the physical world, however, we often argue about *why* something happened, usually because we are looking for someone to blame. When it comes to *why,* there are no facts, there are only perceptions, and all perceptions are shaped by the biases, desires, and intent of the perceiver's consciousness. Once the arguing begins, we get thoroughly distracted, truth falls into oblivion, and no one sees the bigger picture. By simply presenting what is happening today and not arguing about how and why we got here or looking for someone to blame, it is a little easier to see the bigger picture, as well as trends and connections. And right now, I think it would be very useful to see the bigger picture. Once we have that, we can make decisions about what to do or say.

What I write comes from a combination of sources: observation of what is going on in the world for over seventy years, reading, research, intuition, insight, Internet sources, conversations with people who have access to unique information, watching a dozen presidents come and go, a deep understanding of consciousness and the nature of reality, and a penchant for noticing and putting together stories and bits of information that others ignore or skip over.

Do not waste your time reading this if you are only looking for flaws in what I write or if you just want to argue about politics. I am not a politician or a political analyst. I am not someone who specializes in economics or international relations. I am not a scientist or journalist. This is *my* thinking, *my* perception, *my* experience, and *my* observation. I write to share. You might find my writing to be a helpful addition to what you are already thinking, seeing, and knowing. What I write might also upset your applecart. What's the point of reading anything if you're not open to new information and perspectives?

When it comes to our government, we all think we know who is doing what and why they're doing it. We think we understand the immigration issue and the border fight, the Russia collusion story, the financial issues, and what the Democrats or Republicans ought to do. We all have our own ideas about science, global warming and the climate change argument. In writing this, I hope to shake your ideas and perceptions to the point that you end up saying, "Gee...I'm not sure what is going on...but I think it's time to shift my consciousness!"

When this happens, you will be a lot closer to the truth because you are more likely to begin observing events more closely, and that is my goal. Attention to events going on behind the scenes and looming in our future have both an immediate and long-term impact on that future.

Keep in mind that the sign of spiritual maturity is the ability to hold simultaneous, multiple viewpoints that conflict with one another without having to believe or align with any of them. The immature spirit is often characterized by either-or thinking, right or wrong, black or white, and other deeply polarized positions that push them into premature decisions and reactions based on incomplete information loaded with biases. They are unable to *see what is* and do not have the energy to hold multiple positions while working toward something good, beautiful, and true.

Few of us have a complete picture of what is going on. I hope to stir up some deeper thinking or at least a little intelligent conversation, even if it's just a conversation in your own head. And I definitely hope you will become one of those working to expand your consciousness. We're going to need it! ✆

Foreword

ALL CHILDREN GROW UP IN A GIVEN MILIEU AND BELIEVE THAT WHATEVER they're experiencing is normal. This makes it difficult for them to envision anything else because their current normal is the way they think it should be. When you try to tell them something has been lost, they don't understand what you're talking about because they never had it to begin with, so therefore, how could it be lost?

From time to time over the last 30 years I would try to tell my children that something was lost, something was not right in our country. They would pooh-pooh this notion partly because they had never experienced what I was talking about and didn't miss it, and partly because they were perfect results of the social programming that ridiculed, embarrassed, and slapped a conspiracy nut label on anyone who spoke up about what they saw going on. The same tactic was used on those who reported UFOs or contact with ETs. Make people embarrassed and ashamed, label them as a nutcase and they will censor themselves, making the job easy for the Cabal.

What job was the Cabal doing? It was busy taking over the United States so they could implement their own version of planetary governance and finance. Our country with its culture of self-reliance, individuality, and freedom has long been quite successful. It is tough to undermine successful people by confronting them directly. Thus, the Cabal implemented a secretive, long-term, multi-pronged plan designed to demoralize and exhaust the people of our nation and *then* take it over at a point when we were too tired to care.

At first, there were not many signs that something was amiss, and I was not interested in politics or what was going on in the world until my mid-thirties. However, I did notice the increasing poverty. When I was growing up, there were poor people and my family was among them, but there were almost no homeless people. The few that existed were called hobos, and we never saw them in public. Then, very gradually, a few people began living in their cars, or on the street, under a freeway overpass, or any place they could lay their head and not be harassed. Slowly, more and more homeless began to appear. This has been like a boiling frog story in housing. If masses of people had suddenly been thrown out of their homes onto the streets, we would have recognized what was happening and maybe done something about it, but it was an imperceptible change that the media was careful to avoid.

When the subject of homelessness did come up, media did two things. First, they gave it the full Hollywood treatment, and second, they blamed it on the economy. The Hollywood treatment always presented the homeless problem as if it were a movie drama that had an end like all good Hollywood scripts. As for blaming the faceless economy, doing this meant no one had to take responsibility or respond because the economy was not someone you could talk to or go to for help. News reports simply spit out the facts saying the economy was slow, jobs were being lost, prices were increasing without increases in wages, and households needed at least two incomes to hang onto the roof. No one ever pointed out that the economy was a system managed by a few men and women who were manipulating things in ways that resulted in gross inhumanity to others. Perhaps today's children think this is how it always was, but it was not.

I grew up in the 1950s and 60s. Life was different then. My children grew up in the 70s and 80s. They are still growing up. It takes at least 50 years to figure out how this reality system works and learn to make good choices! If it takes a minimum of 50 years to learn the ropes of this reality system, and we start falling apart at age 50, we never get a chance to use what we've learned. We're too busy coping with various diseases and dysfunctions of the body. Why do we have those diseases and dysfunctions? There are many reasons. We have never learned how to take care of the body properly. We don't understand how to use consciousness. We don't take a hand in growing our food or pay attention to agriculture and what it does to our food, nor do we know the difference between real food and fake food. We neither make or take time to exercise, have not been educated to think critically or take responsibility, and have been brainwashed into thinking we have to have a job to survive.

If we take the difficulty of dealing with diseases and a failing body then add this to the belief that we should retire by 65, sit in front of the TV, or maybe go traveling while the young ones deal with things, we never use our hard-earned wisdom at all. Our world is a mess because no one is home consciously mentoring the young ones stepping up to fill our shoes. The kids are running the house! Although it's not as bad as the fox running the henhouse, it eventually becomes a disaster. Young people are easily fooled and corrupted by strongmen.

When I was in my thirties, an older associate asked my husband and I if we could design a circuit board for headphones that would route music to one hemisphere of the brain and information to the other. He said he would help us patent it and sell it. My father-in-law must have asked us four or five times during this process if the man we were working with was to be trusted. We assured him it was all good. We developed the circuit board, built it, and demonstrated it to this man who then patented it in his name only in another state. We were left out completely. I asked my father-in-law how he knew. All he could say was, "He reminded me of a guy I knew once who wasn't trustworthy." This was his wisdom, intuition, and life experience in action.

I love the youthful energy and ideas of young people, but they do not always have the breadth and depth of experience to recognize when they're being used. They often do not have the connections that experience brings. When they do have those connections, they don't always know how to use them wisely and well. The young ones are often unaware of the hidden connections pulling the levers of power behind the scenes.

Think of power as a mantle of responsibility that gets passed from generation to generation. Those in their 60s and 70s who are in the process of handing over their mantles of decision-making power in government, finance, education, medicine, science, business, and other realms need to ask, "Should we be handing over power just as we reach our wisdom? Should we remain active and in charge? How do we avoid and counter the abuse of power by those who have been in power for a long time?"

The constant level of chaos in Washington DC is pushing millenials and the young ones to write off the current form of government altogether. Passing this mantle from old to young at this time means handing the young ones the right to change the republic. If they take on this mantle too soon, if they have not reached their wisdom, if they have never realized the value of a republic, *and* we then drop out of the picture because we've reached retirement age and don't want to bother with the daily challenges of life any more, we will be left to cope with the changes they institute. In addition to changes in the balance of power, finance, food and agriculture, medicine, and energy, it appears we will have to face serious changes in our weather and solar system conditions. Are we ready for the future?

I do not know if we will be able to save our country. We cannot go back to the good old days. We can only move ahead. Ready or not, we will have to adapt. Ideally, we will do so with clarity, excitement, and an eye toward deliberate creation of a better world for all. Trump and his team are driving some of the changes we face, but he is only cleaning up corruption. Without this clean-up, a snowball in hell would have a better chance of surviving...but I am getting ahead of myself. Trump is not the focus, our future is our focus. ⚕

Prologue

I WAS TOO YOUNG TO REMEMBER THE FIRST ELECTION OF EISENHOWER, but I will never forget his second election and the paranoia around Russia and the Communists. I cried at the funerals of John F. Kennedy, Robert Kennedy, and Martin Luther King, Jr.; watched Lyndon Johnson dig us deeper into war in Vietnam; witnessed the public uproar over Watergate; and watched Richard Nixon resign rather than be impeached. I was embarassed by Gerald Ford, agonized over the inability of Jimmy Carter to free the American hostages in Iran, and was appalled by the attempted assassination of Ronald Reagan in 1981. I was angered by George H.W. Bush's bombing of Iraq and Kuwait on my birthday in January 1991, and felt insulted as I watched the Clintons wiggle out of the Savings & Loan Scandal then sail through sex scandals and murders.

I was horrified as I watched George W. Bush be declared president by the Supreme Court after a bungled election, and I was sickened by the way he handled the September 11th tragedy—as if we were all in the 5th grade. I watched him, Dick Cheney, Donald Rumsfeld, and Colin Powell lie through their teeth about weapons of mass destruction in Iraq. I knew instinctively they were all part of the whole plot, and I cried for a month when we attacked those beautiful people. When Bush Jr. went on to sell off every government service that he possibly could before leaving office in his second term, I knew something big was up, something that was probably not going to end well. Meanwhile, Americans began to suffer as the *motive to serve* was replaced by a *profit motive* in many of the institutions sold by Bush.

I had hope for a brief minute when Obama was elected president in 2008, but was quickly disappointed by the continued erosion of our rights and the terrible gutting of our military. We were headed down the path of one poor leader after another, and I was deeply worried.

Obama had not even been elected yet when, in 2008, friends of mine began leaving the country saying they could see what was coming and didn't want to be here for the chaos. They urged me to leave as well. I almost did.

Then I happened to read a book titled *Anastasia.* I went on to read the entire *Ringing Cedars* series of books written by Vladimir Megré. It is a true story that begins with Megré in 1994. He is a ship captain who travels up the Ob River from Novosibirsk, Russia, all the way to Siberia each summer, selling necessities to villages and tribes that live along the river, then making his way back to Novosibirsk before winter sets in. On his way back down the river, he is approached by two old men who ask if they can borrow Megré's crew for a day or two. They want the crew to cut down a ringing cedar in the forest. Megré refuses. They try to explain further. Megré has no idea what a ringing cedar is and says he's already in danger of being caught in ice before reaching Novosibirsk. They warn him that he will need a piece of the ringing cedar to regain his health, but he ignores them and leaves.

Once back in Novosibirsk, he is hospitalized with a serious duodenal ulcer. While recovering, he thinks about the two men who wanted to cut down the ringing cedar. He decides that on his next trip up the river, he will stop and see if he can find the two men again. However, when he gets to that point on his next journey up the river, he finds a young woman waiting for him. She is Anastasia, the granddaughter and great-granddaughter of the two men he met previously. Megré follows her into the forest, discovering that she lives there without a house, eats only what the forest offers, and communicates with all animals. She teaches him about the power of a ringing cedar tree, a fairly rare event in which the cedar signals its readiness to be cut down and turned into chips that will heal people. As it turns out, Anastasia has chosen Megré to be the father of the child she wants! Their relationship begins, and her work begins to unfold in a series of nine books.

In this series, Anastasia shares the fact that her great-grandfather was one of a group of six men who discovered the secret of immortality. Because of their longevity and experience in the world, they became extremely powerful men and had been working for many hundreds of years to get control of the planet. They were using their power to manipulate humanity into subservience. Over the course of Anastasia's life, her great-grandfather dropped out of the effort, leaving only five men driving the ancient program of ruling the world. Anastasia began using her considerable powers to counter the efforts of the remaining five men.

If we explore the idea of ruling the world and where this may have come from, there are several possibilities. One is that the Christian descendants of Abraham have handed their plans to one generation after another since approximately 1800 B.C. Another is that the six men in the group known to Anastasia survived because they had access to ancient Vedic secrets, then moved into modern times and found ways to take charge of men, money, and governments. A third is that an entirely new group of people with dreams of controlling the world have been working steadily to accomplish their dream for the last 250 years. There are also a few stories around claiming that ETs are trying to take over the world. Any way you want to look at it, the idea of controlling the world has attracted at least a few people and groups regularly over the past 3,800 years.

The story of Anastasia is entirely inspiring, but the important point to be made is that on one occasion, Anastasia tells Megré a story about the not-too-distant future in which a man in America who has accumulated many billions of dollars but has lost his spark of interest in life suddenly awakens to love and changes his entire life, working to reverse destruction, bring joy to people, heal the planet, and make the world a better place.

When she is finished with her story, Megré assumes that she made up the whole story and asks if it will really happen. She tells him that it was not an imaginary story, but was a projection from the future, and that although the names and locations will be different, the story would prove to be true. She insisted that the possibility of a good life for people in which positive feelings predominated would happen for us and our planet.

It is curious that we in America now find ourselves led by a billionaire who was part of an elite crowd and who suddenly stepped away from his very comfortable life to become the president of the U.S. in order to confront and remove the rampant corruption that has taken hold around the planet. He didn't need to do it. We don't know why he did it. Maybe it was for fun. Maybe for the challenge. Maybe because he cared. Whatever the reason, he did it. &

1 ॐ

The Setup

MANY YEARS AGO WHEN I FIRST HEARD OF THE ROTHSCHILD FAMILY, I HAD a small vision. At that time, I had just read a piece of the story of Mayer Amschel Bauer. Mayer's father was a goldsmith and money lender who owned a small shop in Frankfurt, Germany where he had mounted a sign with a red shield on it over the shop door. The shield represented the Red Flag (similar to the Antifa flag), which was the emblem of the revolutionary-minded Jews in Eastern Europe. I don't know what those early Jews might have been revolting against, but when Bauer later changed his name to Rothschild, meaning *red shield*, the House of Rothschild came into being. [2]

Rothschild had four sons and together, the five of them had taken over the business of banking. When I read this, I wondered how someone had managed to get all of his children to go in the same direction when I had found the job of raising children to be mostly like trying to herd cats. As I mused about Bauer, what he was like, and what kind of father he must have been, I dropped into an altered state and found myself watching a young Jewish man walking along a street in a place that looked quite German on his way home one evening. He lived in a Jewish ghetto because,

---

2 Des Griffin, *Descent Into Slavery*; Emissary Publications, Clackamas OR. 1996. Pg. 19.

unfortunately, humans always seem to need a group of people to look down on, and in those days, Jews, Gypsies, and Blacks were the targeted groups and were not allowed to live among the general population. As I watched this young man walk toward the ghetto, he encountered a group of five or six boys who immediately began taunting him. They were mean, told him he looked like a pig, said he smelled funny, and ran circles around him as if they were going to attack.

Bauer kept his eyes straight ahead and did not acknowledge the boys at all. He knew better. He knew what the consequences would be if he struck out or even opened his mouth about non-Jewish boys. He just kept walking, but he was hurting inside. As he walked, the hurt took the shape of an iron resolve. Somehow, someday, some way, he was going to have the power and control to rid the world of rude boys who made fun of full-grown Jewish men as if they were animals without pride or feelings. This resolve welded itself to the ancient promise of Abraham that said, "I will make your descendants more numerous than the stars in the sky and the grains of sand on the beach," and thus was born the Rothschild determination to rule the world.

When this small vision ended, I shook myself back to attention in the present world and thought, "Wow! Where did that come from?" I'm not even sure how I happened to come across the Rothschild story because at that time, I wasn't particularly interested in history, banking, or the stuff governments were doing. I didn't know what to do with what I had seen, but I never forgot those scenes.

Years later, around 2012, I was stunned to read the following in David Wilcock's online book, *Financial Tyranny*. "...Mayer could not escape the street urchins whose favorite amusement was to shout, 'Jew, do your duty!'—whereupon the Jew had to step aside, take off his hat, and bow. Having thus entertained the local children, Mayer reached the heavy chains with which soldiers manacled the Judengasse (Jew Street) every night."

Ⅎ

Staying with the Rothschild story, but moving ahead to the creation of a central bank in the form of the Federal Reserve Banking

System, we see persistent efforts to gain control of the world by the Rothschild bankers. Des Griffin quotes Carroll Quigley from *Tragedy and Hope* saying that the bankers were "vitally interested in achieving another far-reaching aim, nothing less than to create a world system of financial control in private hands able to dominate the political system of each country and the economy of the world as a whole. This system was to be controlled in a feudalist fashion...by the central banks of the world [international bankers] acting in concert, by secret agreements arrived at in frequent private meetings and conferences."[3]

Griffin then goes on to describe what happened in the United States, which, back in the early 1800s, was a juicy, up-and-coming nation on the world stage:

> America was unique in modern history...Its uniquely magnificent Constitution was specifically designed to limit the power of government and to keep its citizens free and prosperous...The Big Bankers in Europe—the Rothschilds and their cohorts—viewed the wonderful results borne by this unique experiment from an entirely different perspective. They looked upon it as a major threat to their future plans...

> The establishment Times of London stated: If that mischievous financial policy which had its origin in the North American Republic should become indurated down to a fixture, then that government will furnish its own money without cost. It will pay off its debts and be without a debt [to the international bankers]. It will become prosperous beyond precedent in the history of civilized governments of the world. The brains and wealth of all countries will go to North America. That government must be destroyed or it will destroy every monarchy on the globe.

---

3 Ibid. Pg. 104.

The first documentable evidence of Rothschild involvement in the financial affairs of the United States came in the late 1820s and early 1830s when the family, through their agent Nicholas Biddle, fought to defeat Andrew Jackson's move to curtail the power of that "den of vipers," the international bankers. The Rothschilds lost the first round when in 1832, President Jackson vetoed the move to renew the charter of the 'Bank of the United States' (a central bank controlled by the international bankers). In 1836 the bank went out of business.[4] (Parentheses mine)

The Rothschilds may have lost the first round, but came back to fight again by agitating and supporting the Southern states until the Civil War was sparked. When the South lost, the bankers lost that round as well, but came back again in the early 1900s. Jacob Schiff, head of a Rothschild-owned bank, warned the New York Chamber of Commerce that "unless we have a Central Bank with adequate control of credit resources, this country is going to undergo the most severe and far-reaching money panic in its history." And sure enough, it did.

They pulled one of their favorite tricks—buying up stocks, bonds, and financial assets in great quantity then suddenly dumping them all at once, triggering the Panic of 1907 and a devastating loss of value for those who had invested in those stocks and bonds. Big companies who sold their stocks to hard-working citizens never had to pay back the money that had been invested in them and those investors lost everything. When those companies went belly up, a new company with a new name and new promises of wealth was started using the money pocketed from the recent crisis.

"The purpose for the 'crisis' was two-fold: 1) To make a financial 'killing' for the Insiders, and 2) To impress on the American people the 'great need' for a central bank." [5]

---

4 Ibid, Pg. 33-34.

5 Ibid, Pg. 37-38.

In spite of the 1907 Bankers Panic, there remained a great deal of resistance to handing over control of the nation's money to anyone from the Rothschild group. This resistance continued until 1912 when those businessmen and officials who were opposed to a central bank were invited to be special guests on the maiden voyage of the Titanic. Tragically, the ship went down on April 15, 1912, off the coast of Newfoundland, taking those who were the main opposition to a central banking system with it. The story was spread that they hit an iceberg in foggy weather. Once the opponents were out of the way, the Federal Reserve Banking system was quickly created.

The Fed, as it was called, was created in 1913. It was given the power to print United States dollars, to loan these dollars to the U.S. government, and to collect interest on the loans, which would be paid by the country's hardworking taxpayers. The Fed had no obligation to make decisions favorable to those taxpayers footing the bill because the Federal Reserve was a private company outside the structure of government.

Exactly as predicted, once it was in control, it began pulling serious strings *inside* the government. The first strings pulled were those that pushed the U.S. into World War I. A country at war has to borrow money heavily, and this debt would cement control over the U.S. by the central bankers.

At first, the U.S. resisted getting involved in World War I. However, the Rothschild family wanted to create a Zionist homeland. To do this, they needed land that they could call their own. They had their eyes on Palestine, but it was part of the Ottoman Empire. England had declared war on the Ottoman Empire, so Lionel Rothschild quietly made a deal with England, promising to bring the Americans into the war. In return, he asked that when the war was over and the Ottoman Empire was divided up, the Palestinian land would be given to the Zionists as a Jewish homeland.

It is hard to say what other secret agreements may have been made or what monies may have changed hands in this deal. England was doubtful that America could be brought into the war, but suddenly there was an attack on a British passenger ship, the Lusitania, killing 1,198 people, including 128 Americans. German U-boats were blamed, and propaganda began to fan the flames of vengeance.

Two years later, the U.S. finally entered the war. It was April 1917. Seven months later, Arthur Balfour, England's foreign secretary, wrote a letter to Lord Rothschild promising to support "the establishment in Palestine of a national home for the Jewish people..." His letter became known as the Balfour Declaration. The Rothschild empire now had a home base from which to implement their plans. It was the area of Palestine that is today known as Israel.

Since that time, the plan has been moving forward with its goal of collapsing America, eliminating the rest of the nations of the world, and instituting a new form of global governance. "Their aim was the creation of a One World Government to be ruled over by the *Illuminated ones* at the top."[6]

The new world government the Rothschilds were envisioning was to be more of a benevolent dictatorship that was NOT based on elected representatives who were chosen by sovereign people to manage their laws, trade, and relationships with the rest of the world. Instead, the wealthy would be sovereign and would make decisions for all.

World War I was an effort by the Rothschilds and their cadre of bankers and aligned corporations to firm up control of the U.S., to keep as many nations as possible in debt, and to get rid of the old systems of monarchy and royalty that ruled Europe for hundreds of years. In the Rothschild plan, instead of kings, queens, czars and princes, there would be only nations and their banking systems. Much later, the nations would also be collapsed and there would be only banking systems ruling all in a New World Order of corporate governance and finance. During the war, those royal family members who were not killed outright went underground or faded into the background in order to survive. They would pop up later in an amazing twist of fates.

---

6 Ibid, Pg. 39.

Just before World War I began, world leaders met and, encouraged by the international bankers, decided to suspend the gold standard, leaving them free to print as much paper money as they wished.[7] When the war was over, these leaders met to discuss the plundering that went on in wars. They decided that the best way to end all wars was to have all the nations send their gold to the U.S. where it would be safely stored for the next 60 years. They thought that once the gold was out of the way, they would have better clarity. They could rethink things and decide what to do next to achieve lasting peace.

Between 1920 and 1939, thousands of tons of gold arrived in the ports of New York and California. The United States acknowledged receipt of this gold by printing receipts in the form of bearer bonds that each country could use to redeem their gold when they were ready.[8] Not until years later would it become evident that those controlling the U.S. had deliberately printed bonds with spelling errors and other mistakes on them because they planned to sabotage the attempts of these countries to get their gold back.

In spite of holding gold for a lot of other countries, the fortunes of the U.S. took a turn for the worse. Between 1920 and 1929, the Federal Reserve engineered a series of expansions and contractions culminating in the Great Depression. What began in 1929 as a collapse deepened into a full-blown depression by 1933, bankrupting thousands of investors.[9] Since most of the war had been financed with borrowed money, the U.S. was deeply in debt. The transition of handing financial control of the U.S. to wealthy bankers was complete. The haunting words of Mayer Amschel Rothschild, "Let me issue and control a nation's money and I care not who writes the laws," were now in full play across the land.[10]

---

7 Ibid. Pg. 105.

8 Wilcock, David. *Financial Tyranny*; www.divinecosmos.com. 7 June 2019. https://divinecosmos.com/davids-blog/1023-financial-tyranny/.

9 Griffin, G. Edward; *The Creature from Jekyll Island.* American Media, West-lake, CA.Fifth Edition 2010. Pg. 488-502.

10 There is no original source for this saying, but it has long been attributed to Mayer Rothschild.

⚘

The Rothschilds were not the only group to dream of owning and running the world. In the east, Japan had similar illusions. Their first assault on Korea in 1895 resulted in Korea being fully incorporated into Japan by 1910. It had been looted mercilessly.[11] After their success in subduing Korea, they turned their eye on Manchuria, a northeast Asia province belonging to Russia. They quickly subdued Russia's entire navy and were given Manchuria as their reward. Manchuria had good ports, a railway, lots of land, forests, and minerals, and Japan's intention was to turn it into a modern industrial territory and use it as a base to conquer China. Upon moving into Manchuria, they set up the Center for China Studies,[12] and under the cover of research began cataloging China's wealth. For 20 years, they learned how China worked, who had power, and where the money was.

In 1931, finally ready to invade, the Japanese blew up a stretch of their own railroad in Manchuria. This was a false flag event that they blamed on China.[13] Propaganda designed to fan the flames of war began flowing, and the following year Japan attacked Shanghai. They continued to push inland, and in 1937, the infamous Rape of Nanking began. From there, they pushed on into southeast Asia, the Philippines, Guam, and British-owned Hong Kong. Everywhere they went, they carefully pursued wealthy families, businesses, banks, and even those who were known to be part of the underworld of gangsters, stripping them of their wealth.

The Japanese were so extremely systematic in their looting, extortion, and plundering that when it was over, people described it as pure armed robbery masquerading as war. "He (Hirohito) directed the military to enforce the 'acquisition of strategic materials, the establishment of the self-sufficiency of the occupying army, and the restoration of law and order.' In plain language, acquisition meant armed robbery, self-sufficiency meant forcing local populations to bear the full burden of paying for the

---

11 Seagrave, Sterling and Peggy. *Gold Warriors;* Verso Books, 2005. Pg. 18.

12 Ibid, Pg. 24.

13 Ibid, Pg. 29.

occupation, and the restoration of law-and-order meant using terror to suppress all opposition."[14]

In the looting process, the Japanese confiscated thousands of tons of gold, silver, platinum, and bronze. They collected barrels of jewels and jewelry, artwork of every kind, millions of books and ancient manuscripts, thousands upon thousands of priceless porcelain objects, expensive pottery, and one-of-a-kind anthropological treasures. They looted religious shrines, banks, museums, factories, and even private homes, stripping out wires, plumbing, and anything made of copper, cobalt, nickel, or molybdenum.

All of this treasure was carefully sorted and catalogued through a program called the Golden Lily. From there, it was hidden in 175 vaults scattered throughout the Philippines because Japanese ships could not get through the American blockade to return to Japan. The Japanese intended to recover this treasure after the war, but things did not go as planned.

After their conquests in Asia, the Japanese turned their attention to America, bombing Pearl Harbor in December, 1941. The U.S. had refrained from getting involved in the war going on in Europe. However, when Japan attacked and Germany declared war on the U.S. only three days after Pearl Harbor, the U.S. threw its hat in the ring. The war was on.

When it ended with the Japanese surrender in August of 1945, it did not take the American military long to begin hearing stories of huge amounts of gold, silver, jewels, and other forms of treasure hidden in the Philippines. Publicly, they said nothing, but privately they captured the driver and other staff of one General Yamashita, torturing them until they revealed the location of a dozen of the vaults.

When President Truman was informed of the existence of these vaults and what they contained, he recovered the gold but kept it a secret. "This 'black gold' gave the Truman Administration access to virtually limitless unvouchered funds for covert operations. It also provided an asset base that was used by Washington to reinforce the treasuries of its allies, to bribe political leaders, and to manipulate elections in foreign countries...between 1945 and 1947 the gold bullion recovered (from the

---

14   Ibid, Pg. 45.

Philippines)...was discreetly moved by ship to 176 accounts at banks in 42 countries."[15]

In addition to the black gold that came from the Golden Lily operation in Japan, there was also a great deal of gold looted from the Nazis that was melted down and put into what was unofficially named the Black Eagle Trust. This, too, was kept secret so that no one would be encouraged to come forward and claim it.

Originally, the intent was to use this gold to support the rebuilding of those countries whose infrastructure was destroyed in the war. It was also to be used to recover from natural disasters, fund international projects, and for humanitarian purposes. Instead, it was hidden behind a veil called national security. Said the Seagraves: "What went wrong in the longer term is that the cloak of national security created a situation ripe for abuse. What protects national secrets also protects government officials and their collaborators in the private sector...In the hands of clever men the possibilities were endless...(and) national security made peer review impossible. Who is to supervise clandestine funds, except those who benefit by using them?"[16]

Billions of dollars in gold, silver, platinum, jewels, and art have been in the hands of a few who have no intention of letting go of it. For 70 years, they have used it to buy and sell people, sex, favors, human organs, and power.

This was the setup: 1) Families, groups, nations seeking to rule the world, and 2) a hoard of hidden gold. Who will control it in the future and what will they do with it? The gold may be the elephant in the room as well as the excuse for the fight we see going on around the globe, however, the real aphrodisiac is power, with gold as the drug that makes you believe you have that power. Maybe you do, but it's only temporary and gold is nothing compared to the untapped power of consciousness. ❧

---

15 Ibid, Pg. 3-4.

16 Ibid, Pg. 5.

2 ✍
The Plan

IN ORDER TO SEE THE BIG PICTURE, WE HAVE TO ENVISION THE ENTIRE PLANET, all of her countries, all of her people, and all of her resources as the game board on which the play will proceed. A group of international corporate bankers we will call the Cabal has been seeking to control the world without having to bother with laws or interference from national governments, borders, or the laws set out by each country.

In the mind of the Cabal, the U.S. had to be taken down because it was powerful enough to ruin their plan. Asia would become the new center of power around the globe, with China as the new superpower. The Chinese are very astute and have long centuries of experience in dealing with fools and swindlers. The secret Chinese attitude was that they would let this Cabal make China the new center of world power, and then they would dispose of that Cabal as naïve fools who thought they were going to control China. In sharp contrast, the attitude of the Cabal was that China was the new puppet and was dumb enough to allow themselves to be infiltrated, after which, they would be collapsed, just like the U.S.

Iran and North Korea were to be used as puppets to start wars that would help lower the number of people on the planet. The destruction that occurs during a war would provide continuous need for rebuilding homes, buildings, roads, transportation, and communication systems. Iran and

North Korea could also be used as threats or to intimidate other countries, which was very handy.

A list of some details in the New Word Order plan:

- **Gain control of all banking and financial systems.**
  - Use the banking system to control people as needed.
    - Develop credit scores to control financial compliance and assure a steady flow of money into the system.
  - Set up sources of income from unsuspecting taxpayers.
    - Skim tax money.
      - For pay-offs.
      - For developing and implementing new and hidden forms of energy.
      - For developing new weaponry.
      - For developing proprietary healing technologies.
      - For building underground cities that serve as hidden power centers, command centers, and places of safety or refuge.
  - Produce & sell drugs.
    - Invade Afghanistan to replant major poppy fields.
    - Construct opium processing plants.
    - Ship drugs back to the U.S. through places like Mena, Arkansas with Bill Clinton's help, and across the U.S.– Mexico border with help from Bush Jr., John McCain, and others, all handled by Poppy Bush, whose nickname had nothing to do with being a husband and father.
    - Make the drugs illegal and institute mandatory prison sentences for those caught selling, using, or possessing any illegal substances.
  - Build and license private prisons.
    - Guarantee investors in the prisons a minimum number of prisoners.
    - Force prisoners to work for pennies while working on projects for the government.

- **Develop and extend the flesh markets.**
  - Hire mercenary soldiers.
    - Create secret, private armies.
    - Train and arm them as terrorists.
    - Send them wherever needed, because this circumvents international laws regarding war and invasions.
    - Create false flag events as needed to distract from any real news that might cause people to question what is happening, or that should be known, thought about, or acted upon.
  - Procure sex slaves.
    - Collect through kidnapping or deals with parents.
    - Sell to politicians, bankers, CEOs, Hollywood stars, other powerful people.
  - Develop pedophilia markets.
    - Set up through orphanages, social services, adoption services, child protective services, underground networks.
    - Sell to religious leaders, politicians, bankers, CEOs, etc.
  - Practice child sacrifice to satisfy old gods.
    - Facilitate by kidnapping, especially during chaotic natural disasters, or paying young women to have babies.
    - Sell to those who worship Lucifer.
    - Sell to those who produce adrenochrome-filled blood.
    - Sell to those who prefer human meat.[14]
  - Develop organ markets.
    - Track desirable organs with compatible blood types through blood banks and online programs (23 & Me).
    - Kidnap and murder people in order to harvest their organs.
    - Sell to hospitals and clinics.
    - Sell to wealthy individuals who are in need of a heart, liver, kidney, lung, or other physical material and do not want to wait on a hospital list.

---

14 LocksNewsNetwork. *L.A.'s Elite Cannibal Restaurant Boasts Katy Perry, Meryl Streep, Chelsea Clinton As Members.* Factions of Freedom. 10 January 2018. https://factionsoffreedom.jimdo.com/2018/01/10/l-a-s-elite-cannibal-restaurant-boasts-katy-perry-meryl-streep-chelsea-clinton-as-members.

- **Begin the slow, careful process of moving the center of power from the West to the East (from the U.S. to China).**
  - Find weak people without ethics or morals, put them into power or into agencies, then direct their votes and decisions.
  - Pay them with money, sex, power, children, guns, blood, drugs, or whatever form of payment they ask for.
  - Slowy move manufacturing out of the U.S. starting with steel, then other commodities such as aluminum, rare earth metals, cars, computer chips, computers, cell phones, clothing, tools, small appliances, even specific foods, working steadily to take over these industries, one each year for twenty years.

- **Take over the Middle East and control the oil the world needs, starting with Iraq and continuing with Syria, Lebanon, Libya, Somalia, Sudan, Iran, and Venezuela.**
  - Remove or destroy world leaders who refuse to cooperate or capitulate (e.g. Muammar Gadaffi of Libya, Bashar al Assad of Syria).

- **Gain control of the media and social narrative using Operation Mockingbird.**[15]
  - Put CIA agents into major newspaper companies and other media outlets.
  - Pass laws that make it legal for the mainstream media to print propaganda instead of news, facts, and deep analysis of events.
  - Allow China to buy Hollywood production companies and theaters[16] while engaging in copyright infringement at will in order to:
    - Sell propaganda.
    - Act as an instrument of cultural change.
    - Introduce Luciferian rituals and rules.

---

15 *Operation Mockingbird.* 26 February 2015. https://www.theblackvault.com/documentarchive/operation-mockingbird/#.

16 Berman, Richard. *China is dictating terms to Hollywood.* 1 July 2016. https://www.usatoday.com/story/opinion/2016/07/01/china-censorship-hollywood-communist-party-column/85790002/.

- Use movies as a messaging system that introduces socialist thinking.
- Provide a source of income to the Cabal.
- Provide sources of beautiful people who can be used for sexual payoffs and favors.

- **Develop a hidden network of psychiatrists, psychologists, and therapists who are skilled at:**
  - Splitting a human mind into multiple personalities.
  - Hypnotizing one of those personalities to kill on command.
  - Hypnotizing those personalities to immediately commit suicide on command.
  - Use this psychiatric network to create sleeper cells—individuals who will carry out mass shootings on command.

- **Use false flag events to create pressure to remove the 2nd Amendment, thus getting rid of the right to bear arms.**

- **Control the Presidency, the Supreme Court, the district court system and Congress.**
  - Rig voting machines in order to put chosen people in power.
    - If someone "unapproved" is elected president, assassinate him/her or make his life miserable until his term is up and a new president or judge can be put in place by the Cabal.
  - Set up a sophisticated surveillance program to track what is going on among resistance groups and stay ahead of any challenges to authority.
    - Control the CIA, FBI, NSA, DIA, etc.
    - Set up the Five Eyes program to get around U.S. laws against spying on citizens.
  - Kill anyone who figures out what is going on or gets in the way.
  - Pass laws that weaken the Constitution and peoples' rights while pushing for a Constitutional Convention that would, in effect, gut the main protections/rights it contains by countering them enough to make them irrelevant or inert.

- **Gain control of agriculture, seeds, and the food supply.**
  - Recommended Daily Allowances (RDA) set to barely keep people alive and never achieve robust health.
  - Nutrition levels lowered keeping I.Q. low, emotional instability high, and health marginal-to-poor.
  - Promote a food pyramid that recommends against the critically needed fats that prevent dementia, Alzheimer's, Parkinson's, and obesity.
  - Engineer seeds that will not reproduce in an open-pollinated manner so that they must be repurchased every year.
  - Make it a crime to collect and grow one's own seed from plants grown privately.
  - Promote agricultural use of highly poisonous pesticides, herbicides, and fungicides combined with heavy metals and newer forms of chemicals that interfere with basic biological processes.
  - Create stiff obstacles for organic growers in the form of expensive fees, nuisance inspections, massive amounts of paperwork, etc.
  - Plant harmful bacteria and other organisms in public restaurants that move toward organic foods or that balk at food regulatory practices and fees.
- **Set up international trade agreements such as the Transatlantic Trade & Investment Partnership (TTIP) that can be used to:**
  - Channel money, food, goods, and jobs to various countries as desired.
  - Create shortages as needed anywhere in the world.
  - Undermine every country's ability to be self-sustaining.
  - Continue to destroy the U.S. work force and manufacturing base.
- **Gain control of the medical system.**
  - Develop and control the pharmaceutical system as a major source of income.
  - Make it illegal for an M.D. to recommend any form of natural healing.
  - Price drugs so that Americans are kept poor and sick.

- Force doctors to order a minimum number of prescriptions, surgeries, and other procedures or be fired by the hospital for failure to reach quotas that support the hospital.
- Emphasize treatment with drugs that will alleviate symptoms but never address the underlying cause of a condition so that healing never happens and people continue to take drugs forever.
- Murder natural medicine doctors.
- Murder or imprison scientists who research and support natural medicine or who reveal the truth about vaccines or negative side effects of drugs.
- Murder and obstruct journalists who try to educate people about the value of real healing vs. drugs and surgery.
- Market and spin information about medical experiments and breakthroughs so that their resemblance to the torture methods of Nazi doctors in concentration camps is not obvious.

- **Gain control of the education system and design curricula that dumb down the majority.**
  - Teach *basic* reading and *basic* math, no penmanship, minimal science, and a sanitized version of history so that skills and perception are kept at a minimum.
  - Fast-track those who excel in high school and college into high-paying positions, making sure they absorb and are rewarded for abiding by the principles of a one world, one government, socialist order of control and high-tech development.
  - Teach everyone they need a job to survive, then control the jobs.
  - Make sure people do not know how to survive in nature so they remain dependent on jobs.

- **Create institutions and private foundations that can be used to launder money and promote socialist agendas while serving as slush funds and private pocketbooks for the Cabal.**
  - Clinton Foundation (Q2561, 2872, and Q2586).[17]

---

17 www.qmap.pub. Drop #2561, *There's Been an Active Probe Into Clinton Foundation,* 6 Dec 2018. Drop #2872, *Evidence on Weiner's Laptop,* 22 Feb 2019. Drop #2586, *It's All Coming Out,* 11 Dec 2018.

- Nancy Pelosi's Foundation. (Q76 and Q5)[18]
- The McCain Institute. (Q732)[19]
- Numerous Soros-supported foundations such as MoveOn.org.[20]
- The Clinton Health Access Initiative (CHAI) (a number of investigations are now underway into CHAI money laundering and other illegal practices).
- The Environmental Protection Agency.
- Fund foundations that promote socialist agendas.
  - Ford Foundation.
  - Kellogg Foundation.
  - Pew Foundation.
  - Other foundations.

- **When all of this is up and running well, embark on the 16-Year Plan with its final initiatives:**
  - Collapse as many national borders as possible.
  - Get control of the leadership in several countries in order to use them to threaten the rest of the world.
  - Start wars as necessary.
  - Create massive destruction of cities and towns in Muslim areas, creating millions of refugees.
    - Encourage and even pay millions of these refugees to resettle in other countries, resulting in chaos, collapse of cultures and overwhelmed nations, all of which furthers the goal of

---

18 www.qmap.pub. Drop #76 *Saudi Arabia & Foundations*. Drop #5 *Follow the Money it's the Key*. 5 November 2017. *Nancy Pelosi has a $196 million net worth on a $193,000 senator's salary*. https://www.reddit.com/r/The_Donald/comments/5x32xk/fun_fact_nancy_pelosi_has_a_196_million_net_worth/.

19 www.qmap.pub. Drop #732 *John McCain is a Traitor*, 11 February 2018. Craddick, William. *McCain Institute's Failue to use Donations for anti-Trafficking Purposes Raises Questions*, 8 Mar 2017. https://www.zerohedge.com/news/2017-03-08/mccain-institutes-failure-use-donations-anti-trafficking-purposes-raises-questions/.

20 Eowyn, Dr., List of 206 Organizations Funded by George Soros That are Operating in the U.S. 12 April 2017. https://needtoknow.news/2017/04/list-206-organizations-funded-george-soros-operating-us/.

collapsing nations in order to implement the New World Order.

- Insist on laws that allow Muslim refugees into Christian countries in the hope that war will break out between them.
- Carry out secret agendas for the benefit of the Cabal.
  - Sell top secret blueprints of how to build nuclear weapons to a couple of countries (North Korea, Iran).
  - Supply those countries with uranium (the Hillary Clinton/Uranium 1 Deal).
  - Help Iran and North Korea build nuclear weapons while keeping this very quiet.
  - Publicly label these countries as "rogue" countries who threaten world peace, then force these countries to provoke war.
  - Expand the war to start World War III, which will reduce population and cause prodigious spending on arms as countries take out massive loans, digging themselves deeper into a debtor's hole.
  - When these indebted countries can't pay back the loans, force them to turn over all their natural resources to the banking system, known as *austerity*, leaving the people of the country impoverished and their government hog-tied.

By the 1960s, parts of the Cabal plan were rolling forward, especially Operation Mockingbird. The goal of this operation was to use the media to present only those reports that had the correct biases and were approved by the Cabal. CIA employees were hired in newsrooms where they wrote stories, suppressed certain information, and reported on other journalists. With Operation Mockingbird in full swing, they carefully directed the attention of Americans away from anything of political depth or economic relevance. Then they began setting things in motion to foster the degeneration of American consciousness using food, pharmaceuticals, the education industry, and the medical industry.

The Cabal had control of the banking system, oil, the media, freedom to print unlimited dollars, and a powerful military loaded with weapons. Large segments of the population were corralled in and around cities where hard-working, educated people needing money were willing to show up in this factory or that office at the same time every day, repeating the same behaviors endlessly and doing as they were told. Completely focused on jobs and making ends meet, they were too busy to realize that agreeing to work at those jobs supported further development of the corporate-banking cabal.

As people left farms and rural life in huge waves of migration to cities, global control became much easier. When people move to the city, they lose their connection to Mother Nature along with an entire array of survival skills and knowledge. In the city, everything necessary for people to survive—food, water, land, transportation, and communication—is something you have to buy. Thus, getting money became the single survival skill you needed to know because the fact is that *money is now the root of survival*. As more and more people relied on dollars to ensure survival rather than on self-sufficiency, personal skills, and knowledge of how to work with Nature and animals, we not only lost a certain intrinsic security that stabilized us, we lost clarity and our inner authority. We became more and more *dependent*, a factor that was carefully nursed by those in control.

When Nixon took us permanently off the gold standard, leaving our dollars backed by nothing other than the value of the paper they were printed on, the combination of *1)* Creating a situation in which people needed dollars to survive, and *2)* The ability to easily print and move an unlimited number of paper dollars made it possible to bribe and manipulate anyone anywhere in the world, hidden gold notwithstanding.

To solidify control, however, the trick was going to be gutting the U.S. Constitution and taking full and final control of the United States without her people realizing what was going on. What was needed was a slow and silent coup to infiltrate deeply enough to get the people to gut their own Constitution and make the changes that would insure continued control by the quickly evolving cabal of banks and corporations. &

3 ❧

The Long Coup Begins

THE COUP BEGAN ON A SUNNY AFTERNOON IN DALLAS, TEXAS, WHERE A group of well-hidden people, both inside and outside the U.S. government, carried out the assassination of President John F. Kennedy. It was a huge risk, but it was well-organized and was carried out successfully. Nevertheless, they were as surprised as anyone when they got away with it. Lyndon Johnson stepped into the role of president, and they moved forward slowly, paying people to keep quiet, murdering the few who knew too much or wouldn't shut up, and being very careful lest they make a move that would alert people to their plot or plans.

The string of presidents that followed Lyndon Johnson were problematic for those who were trying to consolidate control and power, but each new president or situation was used as a lesson that helped to develop better strategies for maintaining control.

Martin Luther King, Jr. was next to fall because he was waking up black people to their own dignity and power. Keeping them afraid and angry was a necessary part of the takeover plan because such distrust allowed the hidden controllers to manipulate people into fighting each other.

When John Kennedy's brother, Robert Kennedy, decided to run for president, they used Sirhan Sirhan, one of their mind-control assets hypnotized to kill on command, to dispose of him. When this succeeded, they knew they were onto something big in moving their plan forward. However, after this second Kennedy assassination, they had to pull back and be quiet. There was too much uproar in the country, too much danger of being discovered, and a lot to be integrated in terms of further learning regarding the handling of big moves.

When Nixon was elected, he proved to have ideas of his own. He contacted China and then visited the Chinese, putting another stick in the eye of the corporate-banking cabal who wanted China to remain a dark, mysterious place that could later be used to threaten Americans. When a group of five burglars from Nixon's re-election committee were caught trying to wiretap the Democratic National Committee in the Watergate office complex, Nixon made the mistake of trying to cover it up. After all, it IS illegal to spy on your adversary in a presidential election. Mainstream media blew up the Watergate scandal to monstrous proportions, and the FBI began to investigate Nixon. He countered by asking the CIA to obstruct the FBI investigation—another crime—and eventually resigned rather than face the impeachment process. This resignation provided several payoffs for the Cabal. They were rid of a president who had big plans of his own, and they perfected Operation Mockingbird a little more in learning how to use media quite effectively to crucify someone.

When Nixon stepped down, Gerald Ford finished out Nixon's term with Nelson Rockefeller as his vice president. Rockefeller was a clear insider belonging to the Cabal. Ford was compliant with the corporate-banking group and seemed to be completely ignorant, thus did not pose much of an obstacle.

President Ford was followed by Jimmy Carter. Carter was not one of the insiders in the Cabal group, so they managed him by packing his cabinet and advisors with people who were sympathetic to the growing takeover network of corruption and control that was still taking shape. They also made sure Carter was completely distracted and absorbed by the Iranian revolution and the 52 Americans who were taken hostage and held for over a year.

Carter was followed by Ronald Reagan, who also had ideas of his own. During the campaign, Reagan repeatedly stated he was not interested in George H.W. Bush as his running mate. When Reagan surprised the corporate-banking cabal by winning the nomination, they went into quick action. A group of men in dark suits took Reagan into a private meeting the night of the nomination. When they emerged some time later, Reagan quietly announced that he was going to have Bush as his running mate.

The Cabal plan was to assassinate Reagan and slide Bush into the presidency in a smooth move that no one would suspect. However, Reagan survived the assassination attempt, thwarting the plan. The result was a new plan using a slow poison to destroy Reagan's mind in hopes of declaring him incompetent. It didn't work fast enough, and Reagan made it to the end of his term, albeit with some concern on the part of those of us who were observing what was happening.

Once Reagan was out of the way, the Cabal decided it was time to put one of their own directly into office—George H.W. Bush. He was tall, smooth-talking, and had accumulated name recognition during his time as Vice President. He had also collected a lot of dirt on the people in Washington D.C. and other places in the government during his time in the CIA. Unfortunately, few knew that Bush was not his real name. His real name was George H. Scherff, Jr. He was born in Germany and was the son of George H. Scherff, Sr., a Nazi who had come to America illegally. Once here, Scherff Sr., an accountant, worked for Nikola Tesla. Scherff Jr. often hung around Tesla's lab while his father was at work. Reportedly, Tesla disliked the younger Scherff intensely and did not trust him.[20]

At any rate, the young Scherff was sent to live with Prescott Bush, who then adopted him. Scherff changed his name to Bush and began his long climb to power. He worked in the CIA, including a program known as MK-Ultra, the same mind control program that would eventually produce Sirhan Sirhan.

---

20 From the papers of Otto Skorzeny, German undercover agent who knew Scherff from an early age and who worked with Bush once they came to America.

Bush Sr. was elected handily without anyone realizing that he was part of the group that had taken out JFK. Even after Bush's speech about creating a New World Order, it was a long time before anyone suspected that he was part of the group working to gain control of the U.S.

With the successful insertion of Bush into the presidency, the Cabal began to move their plans ahead ever more quickly. Using their own preselected and groomed candidates for the role of president, they settled next on a young Arkansas governor who had been very cooperative in allowing the Bush family to run drugs through Mena, Arkansas—Bill Clinton.

Clinton was a willing participant in the sex, drugs, murder, and mayhem carried on by the Cabal. Whether he understood it or not at first, Clinton's sexual appetites made him an easy target for blackmail. He didn't seem to mind the risk as long as there were plenty of women and children available for sex. He left the worrying to his wife, Hillary Clinton, who was deeply interested in power and quickly became part of the Cabal group both as advocate and tool.

⚓

Following Bill Clinton's presidency, George H.W. Bush's son became president. Often referred to as Bush Jr., George W. Bush was a spoiled, devil-may-care kid who revealed that he was mostly a puppet when he failed to show up for key appearances on the campaign trail. He knew the election was rigged and felt no need to expend any undue energy. When a snafu involving unclear ballots in Florida delayed the results of his first election, the Supreme Court stepped in to declare Bush the winner over Al Gore. Too late, a recount showed that Gore had won.

Only months into his presidency, and with the ability to avoid accountability for any irregularities, the Cabal was beginning to flex its muscles. And flex it did! They carried out the destruction of the World Trade Center (WTC), which killed 2,300 people, including those in Bldg. 7 who were investigating massive money laundering and corruption in the U.S. government and its financial markets.

Unknown to many people, the countries who sent gold here for safekeeping after WWI were suing the U.S. in an attempt to retrieve their gold because the 60-year holding period had ended. When the U.S. lost the case, it was ordered to return the gold, which was stored in vaults in the basements of the WTC. The gold was to begin shipping on September 12, 2001. We all know what happened instead. On September 11, 2001, the WTC was attacked and exploded, collapsing into piles of dust and rubble. When the rubble was cleared away and the basement vaults opened, they were empty. The entire event was later very aptly labeled the biggest, most dramatic gold heist in the history of mankind.

I confess that I hated George W. Bush. Right from the start I detested his arrogance and lies. Dick Cheney was worse—an outright criminal. Ditto for Donald Rumsfeld. I KNEW there were no weapons of mass destruction, and I could not believe people fell for this story. I KNEW Bush was handing out subtle threats to us when he said, "You're either with us or against us," indicating that we'd better get on board with the invasion of Iraq or we would be thrown into the camp of the enemy and labeled as traitors, terrorists, or enemies of the state. However, I was *not* on board, and sadly, I knew that peaceful or legitimate protest was no longer okay with our government.

Blaming a group of men from the Middle East for the entire Trade Center debacle, Bush Jr., Donald Rumsfeld, Dick Cheney, and others then set about invading Iraq to get control of Iraqi oil. Once they had this oil, they went after Afghanistan to gain control and further develop income from a lucrative drug trade.

Only three weeks after the bombing of the WTC, a 340-page document called the Patriot Act was introduced to Congress and was pushed through practically overnight. It was obvious that the document had to have been prepared long before the trade center bombing because such a comprehensive document could not have been written in the three weeks of chaos following September 11th.

There was nothing patriotic about the Patriot Act. It started the process of gutting the First, Third, Fourth, and Fifth Amendments to the Constitution, damaged the Seventh and Tenth Amendments, took away our protection against unreasonable search and seizure, nixed our right to habeas corpus,[21] defined terrorism as any act that endangers human life and is a violation of federal or state law, and included a provision that anyone who was considered a terrorist could be *disappeared*. It allowed corporations to conduct secret activities using toxic biological, chemical, or radiological material; gave immunity to any law enforcement agencies that engaged in spying on us; declared that any gathering of news or intelligence could be considered illegal at the whim of the government (severely compromising news organizations); created lifetime parole, which essentially made slavery a possibility for an entire lifetime; set huge fines for a whole new array of crimes; made it a crime to use encrypted software in the process of committing a crime, thus using a cell phone or computer could be a crime if you were deemed to be a terrorist; and declared that all your assets could be seized if you were declared a terrorist.[22]

Anyone who has studied the events of September 11 and the World Trade Center will find dozens of facts that do not add up. Rather, they point to a conspiracy boldly carried out. This is also true for many of the later bombings and shootings labeled terrorist events[23] by those running our government and media. Those who poked holes in the mainstream media stories were murdered, destroyed financially, or made to look like paranoid idiots hawking dramatic stories to get attention. The same tactics used to silence those interested in UFOs were used against those claiming that the 9/11 facts did not add up and pointed to a conspiracy at the highest levels of government.

---

21 Habeas corpus requires that we be brought into court within a reasonable amount of time after being detained, that we have a chance to defend ourselves, and are released if there is insufficient evidence to maintain detention.

22 See Patriot Acts 1 and 2.

23 The meaning of the word *terrorist* originally referred to a government that terrorized its citizens and used false flag events to make them comply with unpopular rulings. In the U.S., many terrorist events have been planned and carried out by factions in the Cabal. However, the Cabal-controlled media has successfully deflected all responsibility, pinning blame on individuals they label as terrorists or rogue activists.

For Bush Jr.'s second term, the use of electronic voting machines and a large number of voting irregularities made it clear to those of us who were watching that the corporate-banking Cabal was now fully in control and able to alter our votes to put whomever they wanted into office. I knew that voting machines had been rigged long before information started to surface about the debacle in Ohio. No one wanted Bush Jr., and yet there he was again—president. Using the mainstream media, all questions about the mismatch between exit polls and the voting results were tossed aside as conspiracy theory. It was clear that elections were now a sham and we, the people, were irrelevant.

Immediately, Bush Jr. began the process of privatizing many government services, which, for all practical purposes, gutted them. As private businesses, these services were now subject to profit motives and cost controls, abandoning the population and purpose they were supposed to serve.

I watched as Bush lied and privatized his way through the term, but what really bothered me was that his arrogant, disengaged, screw-you attitudes trickled down and crept throughout the consciousness of our country giving people subtle, non-verbal permissions to lie, cheat, and take advantage of others. Win-win was not part of his approach to life.

Finally, in 2008, just before leaving office, Bush Jr. and his friends in the Federal Reserve engineered a massive financial collapse that allowed them to hand out trillions of dollars to their buddies in the banking system while also collecting a number of homes and properties that were handed over in a wave of thousands of mortgage foreclosures. These properties were later used by banks to pay down our debt to the Chinese, giving them ownership and control of a good deal of land in cities in the U.S.

During the Bush Jr. years, the term *conspiracy theory* began to be heard a lot. It is a valid term that comes from academia. There are two theories of history and how events unfold. One is called the *Accidental Theory,* and the other is the *Conspiratorial Theory.* The Accidental Theory maintains that events in history, such as wars and revolutions, occur spontaneously for no apparent reason, and kings or presidents are powerless to intervene. The Conspiratorial Theory says that events occur by design, for reasons that are not generally made known to the public, and, in fact, are usually triggered or caused secretly without ever being announced.[24]

As the presidency of Bush Jr. slowly revealed, there *was* a Cabal of crooks operating in the U.S., but for the vast majority of American people who were struggling to make ends meet, were educated to do as they were told, were too sick to take action, too depressed to care, or too politically naïve and disengaged, the idea that their democracy was a charade was too much to deal with. For a long time it was easier to just watch the news and believe what they were being told because this required no engagement other than observation from a distance.

It was during the presidency of George W. Bush that I attended a briefing in Texas explaining that there was a plan to collapse the United States, destroying its power and bringing the level of income and education down to the level of third world countries. We would then become part of the North American Union, a new power-state combining Canada, the U.S., Mexico, and Central America. The North American Union would then create a compact with a new South American Union, and the two entities would become The Americas, a single political and financial region based on Christianity and having a single currency. European nations would also be coalesced into a single European Union, which would eventually unite with Africa to form a EurAfrican power region based on Islam and having a single currency—the Euro—of its own. China-Australia would become a third power block based on a combination of Buddhism and Hinduism, also having a single currency, the Yuan. From the Cabal point of view, these three power regions with their competing religions and currencies would be the perfect setup for ongoing wars that would keep the population down to a manageable level. The production of guns and war equipment would keep people working and provide money to the people at the top who were planning to control all this. &

---

24 Epperson, Ralph. *The Unseen Hand, An Introduction to the Conspiratorial View of History*. Publius Press, Tucson, AZ. 1985. Pg. 6-7.

4 &

The Long Coup Heats Up

WHEN THE BUSH JR. PRESIDENCY ENDED, MY RELIEF WAS IMMENSE, HOWEVER, the relief was short-lived. Bush was followed by Barack Obama. I listened to the campaign rhetoric and thought he sounded quite intelligent and very right about what we needed. However, I kept having a subtle resistance to him that I could not pinpoint. I kept pushing that resistance aside.

Although there was a lot of excitement about having a first black president, I was not interested in his color. I was interested in him beating John McCain. My skin crawled every time I watched or listened to McCain. I didn't know much about him, but my intuition as a human and as a woman could not be talked down to a calm appraisal. Everything in me screamed, "Traitor, liar, cheater…" long before these characteristics were publicly revealed by the *Veterans Today* website.

For a while after the Obama election, I clung to hope, but he did nothing to help correct the worsening situation in our country. Under Obama's direction, a purge of top military personnel was carried out,[23] dumping a few people that I personally knew were good people and

---

23 Editorial: *Obama's Military Coup Purges 197 Officers in Five Years.* Investor's Business Daily. 29 Oct 2013. https://www.investors.com/politics/editorials/197-military-officers-purged-by-obama/.

cheating them out of all the retirement benefits they had earned over many years. It took me some time to figure out why such good people were being taken out. Then I realized that anyone who looked or sounded like they were ethical, or anyone who would not follow orders to commit a crime or open fire on the American people, were the ones being dumped.

Sometime during Obama's time in office, we began to hear the term *deep state*. The term *deep state* originated long ago in Turkey. "In the United States, the term *deep state* is used in political messaging to describe collusion and cronyism that exists within the political system. Some analysts believe that there is a 'hybrid association of elements of government and parts of top-level finance and industry that is effectively able to govern the United States without reference to the consent of the governed as expressed through the formal political process,' whereas others consider the deep state to encompass corruption that is particularly prevalent amongst career politicians and civil servants."[24]

Regardless of label, more and more people were beginning to understand that there *was* a Cabal of politicians, elite bankers, and multi-national corporations that controlled business around the world and used power to further their own interests and rights rather than the interests and rights of the people of the countries in which they operated.

Lately, the terms *cabal*, *shadow government* and *deep state* have been used interchangeably. They all refer to powerful agents and corporations that pull the strings of power in government. When they succeeded in getting corporations classified as *persons*, they were able to qualify for all of the unquestioned protection that is granted under the phrase "human rights." To understand the shocking effects of this accomplishment, which was then followed by the passing of laws that gave them immunity from all responsbility to society or the planet, watch the documentary *Hot Coffee*. It is a stunning revelation of the degree to which the corporations have been replacing the power of government.

---

24 Wikipedia, *Deep State in the United States*. 26 May 2019. https://en.wikipedia.org/wiki/Deep_state_in_the_United_States/.

Obama did nothing to stop or reverse the National Defense Authorization Act, which promotes the conditions of a police state. He did nothing to stop the renewal of the Patriot Act, and he pushed through the ObamaCare program, forcing people to buy insurance many didn't want while punishing those who refused to sign up. Prices were high, and deductibles were higher than the amounts many people spent on medical expenses in an entire year. I thought he should have spent his time coming up with something useful for those who really needed help with medical expenses, or better yet, begin telling the truth about what was happening with the lack of nutrition in the food system and change *that*.

The birth certificate issue would not go away, and I had enough experience to know that where there's smoke, there's usually fire. When Loretta Fuddy, the woman who authenticated Obama's birth certificate, was the only passenger to die in a strange private plane crash a few yards off the coast of Hawaii,[25] I knew something was up.

It bothered me that the general health in this country was so poor. It bothered me even more to know that the reason for such poor health was the poor diet of factory foods that contained no real nutrition. The body must rebuild itself every day. It needs high-density nutrition to do so, but the things people were eating contained no amino acids, minerals, or vitamins. Instead, we had sugared chemicals that *looked* like food. People who ate this stuff were plagued by fatigue, fuzzy thinking, and irritability. It was a racket.

 The agricultural system was growing mostly corn and soybeans for animals or fuels instead of top quality, nutrient-dense food for people. The fake chemical food caused serious inflammation and degeneration. People no longer had any food wisdom, so they ate whatever was available on grocery store shelves. When problems began to show up in the body, they ran to doctors who prescribed expensive drugs with outrageous side effects, or put them in hospitals for terrible surgeries. There was never any

---

25 Hagmann, Doug. *What are the chances? The mysterious death of Loretta Fuddy*, 13 January 2014. https://canadafreepress.com/article/what-are-the-chances-the-mysterious-death-of-loretta-fuddy/.

true healing or rebuilding of the body, just a continuous drain of money going into the pockets of the medical/pharmaceutical industry.

This was a huge source of income for the Cabal. When they realized that tens of thousands of people were abandoning conventional medicine and turning to better food and natural healing agents, they began killing doctors who supported and practiced natural medicine. As of the date of this writing, more than 90 holistic doctors have been murdered over the past several years.[26] Some have been shot, some disappeared, some stabbed, others were hanged, suicided, thrown out of high rise windows, poisoned, or killed with the gun that causes a massive heart attack in a perfectly healthy individual.[27] I knew two of these doctors. One was my personal doctor, Nicholas Gonzalez, and the other was a good friend who operated a clinic in Minnesota and wrote a small newpaper column on natural healing.

Obama prosecuted twice as many whistleblowers who were trying to tell us that something in government was very wrong, and he did nothing about the increase in the rate of false flag events. What began slowly in 1993 with the first bombing of the World Trade Center, then went a couple years to the bombing of the Murrah Building in Oklahoma, and then to the Columbine School shooting in 1999, suddenly became a regular occurrence as the list below shows.

- 2/26/1993 – World Trade Center #1, New York, NY – 6 killed/1,000+ injured; Ramzi Yousef

- 4/19/1995 – Murrah Building, Oklahoma City, OK – 168 killed/600+ injured; Timothy McVeigh

- 4/20/1999 – Columbine High School, Columbine, CO – 13 killed/20 injured; Eric Harris, Dylan Klebold

---

26 Elizabeth, Erin. *Unintended Holistic Doctor Death Series*. 12 March 2016. https://www.healthnutnews.com/recap-on-my-unintended-series-the-holistic-doctor-deaths/.

27 Reality Decoded. *CIA Secret Heart Attack Gun*. 21 July 2018. https://www.youtube.com/watch?v=vYu9ja2ysso/.

- 9/11/2001 – World Trade Center attack #2, New York, NY and Washington, D.C. – 2,996 killed/6000+ injured; Arab pilots

- 4/16/2007 – Virginia Tech, Blacksburg, VA – 32 killed/23 injured; Seung-Hui Cho

- 11/5/2009 – Fort Hood, TX, Military Base – 13 killed/30 injured; Nidal Hasan

- 7/20/2012 – Batman shooter, Aurora, CO – 12 killed/70 injured; James Holmes

- 12/14/2012 – Sandy Hook School, Newtown, CT – 27 killed/0 injured; Adam Lanza

- 4/15/2013 – Boston Marathon – 3 killed/200+ injured; Tamerlan & Dzhokhar Tsarnaev

- 9/16/2013 – Navy Yard, Washington, D.C. – 12 killed/3 injured; Aaron Alexis

- 5/25/2014 – University of California at Santa Barbara – Isla Vista, CA – 6 killed/14 Injured; Elliot Rodger

- 12/2/2015 – Inland Regional Center, San Bernardino, CA – 14 killed/22 injured; Syed Farook, Tashfeen Malik

- 6/12/2016 – Pulse Nightclub, Orlando FL – 49 killed/53 injured; Omar Mateen

- 10/1/2017 – Las Vegas massacre, Las Vegas, NV – 58 killed/851 injured; Stephen Paddock

- 11/5/2017 – First Baptist Church, Sutherland Springs, TX – 26 killed/20 injured; Devin Kelley

This list only goes through 2017, but the attacks have continued through 2018 and 2019 to the present.

After a while, a pattern became clear. A shooting would occur, and then there would be an immediate clamor for gun control from a few politicians. Other patterns also began to surface. Most of the shooters ended up killing themselves or being killed instead of taken alive so we could hear their story. Those who weren't killed were hauled away (Dzhokhar

Tsarnaev and James Holmes), and no one from the press was allowed to interview them. Two of the shooters, James Holmes (Batman shooting) and Adam Lanza (Sandy Hook), were reported to be the children of men who were scheduled to testify in the LIBOR price fixing investigation, but whose testimony was either not given or was given in an untimely and possibly useless manner because of the personal tragedy each was going through at the time of the shootings.

Another piece of the pattern that emerged was that everyone who carried out a shooting had been in touch with the FBI or CIA, or had been in psychiatric treatment for some time, or both. Of 350 million people living in the U.S., how was it that the FBI happened to be working with, or watching, the handful of individuals who turned into mass shooters? As for the psychiatric connection, I was aware of a very secret network of psychiatrists and psychologists who worked for the Cabal and kept an eye out for individuals who would make excellent candidates for splitting and reprogramming.

Once a candidate was found, they would be hypnotized slowly and repeatedly, gradually building an entirely different, alternate personality capable of carrying out stunning acts of violence with absolutely no awareness of what they'd done, and often with the command to commit suicide as a conclusion to their violence. Drugs, sexual predation, and violence were used to help with the destabilization and splitting of the individual's mind, but once the signal code had been embedded in their consciousness, they were a sleeper cell ready to awaken on command and carry out their programming.

Over the course of many years of counseling people around the world, I worked with a half-dozen people who had been subjected to this kind of destabilization and erasure of memory, yet who had somehow been able to recover some or all of the split-off parts of the self and rebuild themselves. I was aware of bits and pieces of this sort of thing, but I did not put it all together until the Navy Yard shooting in 2013.

Let me digress for a moment to say that over the course of 40 years of living and working with intuition, there developed something I called *trigger words* and *window views*. Someone would be talking about something and, for whatever reason, they would use a word that triggered the opening of a window in consciousness through which I could view an entire scene. The scene would usually be related to whatever we were talking about and would provide additional information and background —historical or present day—that provided deep insight into the subject of discussion, the individual I was talking to, or the situation being talked about.

I happened to be listening to the radio as the very first reports of the Navy Yard shooting were coming out. I cannot say exactly what trigger word I heard, but suddenly a window opened providing a view of the entire situation along with intuitive knowing and a full-blown vision of the shooter, the way his consciousness had been tampered with, the psychological connections, and the psychiatric network operating in our country. I knew the reason for the shootings (usually to create fear), the goal (gun control, distraction from something else that was going on in our country, or a warning against betraying the Cabal), that there would be more shootings, and that they would successively worsen.

The effort was on to gut the Second Amendment and take away our guns. If the Cabal could make it illegal to own a gun, the rest would be a cake walk for them. Our hands would be tied, we would be unable to defend ourselves from the enemies within, and the nation would collapse under the pressure of rules designed to undermine the Constitution.

As it was, none of the decisions coming out of Washington, D.C. ever seemed to respond to what the American people wanted. Nothing made sense for *us*. It wasn't just the spreading of Globalism's New World Order, it was that the rule of law was slipping away, replaced by the whims of whoever was in power.

By this time, my intuition was screaming that something was rotten, bad to the bone in our country. The whole picture still wasn't clear, and there were few who seemed interested in putting that picture together, except for a few internet sites that were branded as conspiracy theorists or troublemakers.

Americans seemed content in their ignorance. They did not realize that they were being fed with food that had no nutrition in it; vaccinated with mycoplasmas, retroviruses, and heavy metals; sedated with fluoride in their water; and distracted with movies and television. They were being herded into Hollywood hero worship on one hand and fear on the other by the many terrorist attacks against them—attacks that were always made to look like they were coming from outsiders. They were being handed a line of propaganda that would have made the KGB proud, healed with pharmaceuticals that kept them ill, educated for stupidity and helplessness, indoctrinated into deep biases of racial and religious prejudice, and stirred to senseless rage using those same racial and religious attitudes.

"Isn't anybody going to stand up and say something?" I asked myself again and again.

However, when I tried to say something to my family, they called me "Alice" after some character they'd seen in a movie. I knew that saying something had to be done by more than one person, and it would have to be an entire group that had some actual power. The corruption was everywhere, it was too big, and too entrenched to be dealt with by just one, two, or even a dozen people. Those who spoke up or tried to expose the truth of what was going on ended up murdered. ౭

5 &

Ms. M and the Request for Proposals

AT THE TIME OF MY DIVORCE IN 2008, I TOOK ON LILY HILL FARM BY MYSELF for the first time, along with a ton of debt. I struggled to make ends meet and nearly lost the place several times. A couple of years into that struggle, I happened to meet a man named Stan at a dinner in Kalamazoo. We began talking, and I learned that he had once worked for Donald Trump handling real estate dealings.

Stan knew a lot about business and real estate and tried to coach me to expand my thinking about Lily Hill Farm. One day, he brought me a brief paper and asked me to read and evaluate it. It was one of the most poorly written papers I ever read. It was a Request for Proposals (RFP) that was full of spelling errors, bad grammar, and sounded completely outlandish. He got it from a friend…who got it from a friend…who got it from a friend…

It looked like someone had taken notes of a verbal conversation and tried to reconstruct it as an RFP. The request was asking for proposals that would start a well-thought-out business, would put people to work and pay them enough money so they could pay taxes that would help both the government and the middle class. A woman I'll call "Ms. M" was offering to fund such projects, and she also wanted to be part of the project so that some portion of the profits could be funneled back into the initial fund to be used for another project, thus helping a lot of entrepreneurs as well as helping America get back on its feet financially.

Stan had been a Marine, was educated as a Christian fundamentalist minister, and was now totally in love with business. He had connections all over the U.S. and had also awakened to the potentials of consciousness and intuition. This awakening left him very aware and concerned about the reality of our situation in the U.S. He, too, wanted to help the situation in our country, and he saw something in Ms. M's RFP that he just had to check out.

In his typical fashion, he was not willing to do business with someone he hadn't met and evaluated face-to-face. The name behind the RFP was a woman who lived in Washington, D.C., so he climbed in his car, drove to D.C., and found the woman. He introduced himself, said he was interested in submitting several proposals, and wanted to know the story behind the RFP. He ended up spending the weekend in meetings with her and came away with an amazing story.

She was the granddaughter of a man who had been a trusted senior treasury official or accountant for Ferdinand Marcos, president of the Philippines. Marcos was in possession of some of the bearer bonds[30] that had been issued years ago to countries that sent gold to the United States. Marcos also knew that the Japanese had buried gold at a number of sites in the Philippines. When the U.S. won the war with Japan and eventually found out about the gold that was buried in the Philippines, they went to Marcos and demanded to know where the gold was hidden. Marcos refused to tell them. The Americans claimed that because *they* had beat Japan, it was *their* gold now.

They haggled back and forth for a while, but when Marcos stood his ground, the CIA threatened to remove him. He refused to budge and did not believe they would be able to unseat him. However, the CIA fomented

---

30 According to Wikipedia, a *bearer bond* is issued by a business entity, such as a corporation or government. It is different from the more common type of investment security bond in that a bearer bond is unregistered. No records are kept of the owner or the transactions involving ownership. Whoever physically holds the paper on which the bond is issued owns the instrument.

one of their infamous rebellions. Marcos was made to look totally corrupt, and subsequently, they put Corazon 'Cory' Aquino in his place. Marcos fled to Hawaii where he was slowly poisoned by hidden agents. He died not long after.

However, right before he was removed from power, Marcos gave some of the bonds to one of his most trusted accountants—the grandfather of Ms. M. The grandfather then moved his entire family to the U.S. and began a lawsuit to force the U.S. to turn over the gold it was holding illegally. The grandfather died before the case was settled, so Ms. M's father took up the cause. He, too, died before it was settled, so Ms. M took up the cause—and she won.

Because of the amount of interest that had accrued on the bonds in her possession, Ms. M was now in charge of a very large sum of money that was approaching nearly a trillion dollars. She began trading in the very exclusive world of the international currency markets and was planning to use the proceeds to fund her projects. Her stated purpose was to help the U.S. return to solvency and to rebuild the middle class.

Stan wrote up three projects and put the budgets together, one of them being to develop Lily Hill Farm along the lines he and I had previously discussed. He submitted them and was notified several months later that all three proposals had been accepted. Ms. M communicated that of the nearly 300 proposals received, she had chosen 25 as her top projects. Of those 25, she was going to select the top 12, and of those 12 she was going to start work immediately with the top three. Two of Stan's projects were in the top three, and one of those was the Lily Hill Farm project. Her only criticism was that the budget was too low. "Could you increase the budget to $100 million?" she asked. We complied and then waited.

There had been several assassination attempts against Ms. M during the time she was in court fighting for the return of the gold and she was extremely elusive because of this. She never spent more than a few moments on the phone, usually called from airports as she moved around the world, and often spent long periods hiding in China or the Philippines in order to stay out of harm's way. Finally, we heard from her. She was ready to begin. In a phone conversation with her, Stan mentioned that he would like to submit yet another proposal, this one involving a friend named Jon who planned to build a resort and education center that would help bring people into a new, more awakened, more self-sufficient future. Ms. M curtly replied that Jon was part of the Cabal and hung up! Jon was not part of the Cabal, but Ms. M erased all of the emails and contact numbers Stan had been given, and we never heard from her again.

About this same time, a character named Drake appeared on internet radio shows talking about the efforts of a group of patriots to "end the corruption and take back the country" in a new 4th of July revolution. He said that a number of states in the U.S. had filed papers in the international court of The Hague to become sovereign nation-states. This would allow them to withdraw from the U.S. corporate body and make it possible for those states to return to some kind of alignment with the Constitution of the original U.S. Republic and its Bill of Rights.

Drake sounded very down to earth and well-educated when it came to U.S. history and constitutional law. He reported that a number of people inside the Pentagon were preparing to have U.S. Marshals arrest a large number of corrupt officials in government and banking. They were going to shut down the banks, the internet, and the borders for three days while they made the arrests, and Drake was making this announcement (June 2012) in an effort to give people time to prepare, and to avoid any panic. No specific dates were given other than "soon," but the 4th of July came and went and nothing happened.

When I heard Drake, I was surprised that anyone was talking openly about such plans. I wondered how he was still alive. Political correctness had overtaken everyone after the World Trade Center disaster, a legacy of Bush Jr. This political correctness felt like a weird concoction of 1) consciousness being awakened a little, 2) greater awareness of the need to do something good for the world while, 3) slipping deeper into corruption, selfishness, and greed throughout our political and financial systems. The whole mess was a lot of doublespeak—people saying they were doing something for the good of all when it was obvious they were doing something out of greed, fear, or orders from above that left them no choice and wasn't good for anybody. It was a time of "get on the (corrupt) bandwagon or get out of the way and shutup."

When nothing came of all the talk, I was disappointed but not surprised. I was afraid of revolution, but I was hoping for some positive change. Once again, I concluded that the network of corruption was too big, too entrenched. I felt it would take an act of God to fix things. Although nothing happened on that 4th of July, Drake was a sign that others were seeing what I was seeing and that perhaps things would slowly begin to move in the right direction. As I was to learn later, they began quietly moving in a new direction much earlier—shortly after the 9/11 disaster in 2001—and really began to pick up steam in 2009.

In the summer of 2009, a couple of men were arrested in Italy for trying to enter Switzerland with fake U.S. bonds worth $134 billion. These were some of the same bearer bonds issued by the Federal Reserve in return for the shipments of gold sent to the U.S. back in the 1920s. The men arrested were representatives from a group of Indonesian families known as the Dragon Family. Due to the amount of publicity given to the arrest and these bonds, Neil Keenan, a businessman who held a special power of attorney for the Dragon Family gold, became a person-of-interest to a man who wanted to get his hands on a few of these bonds.

Eventually this man, Daniel Dal Bosco, was introduced to Keenan and managed to create enough trust to hold some of the bonds. However, he took off with them. Keenan was furious as this posed both a deep embarrassment to him and a large loss to the Dragon Family members who had trusted him to hold the bonds until he could place them.

Keenan prided himself on his integrity and business skills. He vowed to fix the situation and restore the Dragon Family's trust in him. As he dug into the situation, however, he ran into a hornet's nest of lies, corruption, double dealing, and stone-walling around something called the Global Collateral Accounts. As he learned the true history of the bonds, what happened to the gold sent to the U.S. after World War I, and the amount of plundered gold hidden by the Japanese in the Philippines and Indonesia, he realized that elite bankers had confiscated as much gold as they could get their hands on and had no intention of honoring the bonds or giving it back. Tons of the yellow metal were being used as collateral to back the Global Collateral Accounts, which were carefully hidden and controlled by the Western banking system. The banking system was no longer exchanging anything of real value when loans and transactions were made. They simply entered someone's name into their computer, assigned the requested numbers of zeroes to the loan, set up the interest rate, and began to collect. It was all done with imaginary numbers. No gold, silver, or dollars were ever at risk and nothing real backed the loan. The only one who stood to lose anything was the poor sucker who took out the loan.

By 2011, Keenan, originally struggling with the larceny of a few bonds, realized he was now struggling with the entire Western banking system and the entrenched corruption that was everywhere. He hosted a secret meeting of representatives from 57 countries, many of whom had discovered that they each were being squeezed by the U.S. for $10 million here or $20 million there and who wanted to do something to stop it. The meeting was held in Monaco on an elegant yacht, but it was crashed by one of the Rockefellers and his goons who tried to muscle their way in. There was a serious confrontation, and the Rockefeller contingent was thrown out. However, Rockefeller and his goons took to the air in helicopters and went after the boat, only giving up when someone ordered fighter jets from their home country to come after them.

When the meeting on the yacht ended and everyone returned home alive, word got around quickly that they had survived the secret meeting. Suddenly the number of countries who wanted to be part of the group increased to 180 countries. As a result of this meeting, Keenan filed a trillion-dollar lawsuit against the Federal Reserve.

I was astounded—and then everything seemed to fade to black. Keenan withdrew the lawsuit to "rewrite technical details," and nothing more happened. There was no more talk about ending corruption, whether in the U.S. or anywhere else. When Drake also disappeared, I assumed the group of patriots leading the efforts to take back the country had been infiltrated and their plans thwarted. Probably they were all dead. By early 2013, it appeared that all was lost, but this was not the case. The group that originally met in Monaco had morphed into something else, something that would not become apparent for a few more years. ॐ

6 ❧
The Trickster Setup

AS OBAMA'S SECOND TERM WAS DRAWING TO A CLOSE, WE WERE FACED with two new candidates—Democrat Hillary Clinton or Republican Donald Trump. When I first heard Trump was going to run for president, I thought it was a joke. I was embarrassed for him and was sure he would lose. However, he persisted, and when he wasn't rattled by hecklers or spouting street talk, he made good sense.

Somewhere in the middle of the 2016 U.S. election campaign, one of my contacts who was directly working for Neil Keenan mentioned that Trump had been *asked* to run for the presidency by those in the military who, with Drake, had originally planned to arrest corrupt officials back in 2012. They were quietly backed by those who attended the meeting in Monaco, as well as those from the old nobility who had gone underground at the time of World War I. All of them, plus the Dragon Family, had come to very similar conclusions—the world was not working for the common man, and this presented a dangerous situation. I understood this immediately. Although the old royal families had always engaged in a certain amount of corruption, they made sure that the common man had a decent life, was paid good wages, and was able to enjoy the life he loved. That way, the nobility could mostly go about its business unhindered.

They had learned over time to share the wealth or there could be severe repercussions or even revolutions against royal families and wealthy elites.

Those newly rich and drunk with power in the relatively younger and less-wise U.S. did not hold this "share the wealth" attitude. Their approach to power and wealth was fearful, selfish, greedy, tight-fisted, and brutal. Those with a longer history of power and wealth knew better. They knew that this approach could not be maintained. They were concerned.

Little by little, the people I was watching, reading, or listening to began to say Trump was sincere and honest. Maybe he was, but what I noticed was that he was a street fighter, someone who was not easily fooled, didn't care if he had to skirt social rules, was going to punch back, call names, hit below the belt if he had to, but had enough integrity to keep his word once he gave it. For some reason, I liked this street fighter view of him. Long ago, I had been double-crossed by some really smooth-talking, elegant, lying politicians and had come to detest such people.

Gradually, reluctantly, I knew at the intuitive level that we had to elect Trump or our country and our way of life would be lost.

As the campaign went on, I happened to see a video[31] reporting that Hillary Clinton had a massive meltdown after an interview with Matt Lauer in which she exclaimed angrily that if she lost the election, they "would all hang." I thought this was an extraordinary statement that hinted at something extremely grave. What was she doing in the corners and closets of her life that she would make such a statement? And who else was involved?

I wanted a woman president, but not Hillary. During the debates, I noted that she responded to the many challenges from Trump by attempting to turn everything Trump said about *her* back onto Trump himself. This was a psychopathic trait that bothered me. She struck me as having an inability to reply honestly and directly, or to take responsibility. She didn't have anything new or creative to say, just a lot of empty promises that

---

31 Still, Bill. *NBC Crew – Crooked Hillary's Massive Meltdown at Commander-in-Chief Forum*. The Still Report #1271, 17 October 2016. https://www.youtube.com/watch?v=_NfFAaPZqs8/.

sounded like all the empty promises of all the political candidates of the last 50 years before her, and I couldn't get her statement about hanging out of my mind. When Trump won, I could see, hear, and feel the utter shock of those who never thought she would lose. They demanded a recount, but it came out that Trump won more votes than originally thought.

৵

As Trump's first year proceeded, I was stunned by the constant attacks on a sitting president and dismayed by what looked like nothing changing, nothing new or innovative happening. This was because it was a classic Trickster setup—you never see it until afterwards. The Trickster setup starts with an a very difficult problem. This problem was the fact that a massive network of criminal corruption had taken root in our government and grown to the point that our republic was gone, the democracy was no longer working, the government was bankrupt, and our country was looked on with contempt by other countries around the world.

In the Trickster setup, in order to resolve the problem, the hero or heroine has been cast into a suppressed, slave-like position (similar to Cinderella) and must waken to the problem and make a difficult choice or take a serious risk. On the one hand, someone beckons the hero (us) to take what looks like a normal, smooth, and familiar path full of promises of relief. This was the choice offered by Hillary Clinton. On the other hand, a man in a clown suit with bright orange hair beckons us to take what looks like a risky and completely unfamiliar path full of contradictions, uproar, and ridiculously impossible challenges. This was Trump—and in a stunning upset, we chose Trump, the clown with the orange hair!

Did we know what the outcome of such a choice would be? No. Did we have any idea what we were doing? No. Did we have a clue what we set in motion? No.

Of course, as often happens in a Trickster setup, once the path has been chosen, the hero/heroine goes through a period of uncertainty, back-pedaling, and chaos. This tests the hero's resolve. And so it was with us. The election was over and the test began.

First, there was uproar when Trump refused to divest himself of his companies, leading to charges that he was going to use his position as president to profit his businesses. Then came the charge of Russian collusion and the Fusion GPS dossier full of salacious accusations about Donald Trump's personal, sexual, and business dealings. Then there were charges that he was inept and a liar. We watched as he filled key positions with people from Goldman Sachs, implying that the corruption would continue and nothing was really going to change.

Then there were charges that he was mentally unfit. A couple of eager-but-foolish psychologists diagnosed him with personality disorder without ever meeting with him on a face-to-face basis—a *major* mistake for a professional psychologist. Using all the power and backing of their profession, they presented the diagnosis as if it were a valid psychological diagnosis, not just one guy calling another guy crazy.

Some of Trump's appointees were accused of lying under oath or of having serious conflicts of interest. A few resigned, creating a lot of turnover, and all the while, the accusations and false narratives spewing from mainstream media kept increasing in volume.

For months, there was sweating, hand-wringing, and secret worries that we made the wrong choice. For months it looked like nothing was happening and nothing had changed. To make things more difficult, mainstream news increased the volume of unfavorable reports, directing a steady barrage of accusations against Trump, insisting that his presidency was a terrible mistake.

As part of the Trickster setup, all of this equates to the test that follows the new choice or decision to change your life. When everyone around is screaming that you have made a terrible decision, that you're an idiot and you have ruined everything, the test is to see whether you can stand in your truth, keep your eye on a goal that can't quite be seen, and quietly march to the beat of your own drum. If you succumb at this point, you're in for another, deeper round of punishing lessons that will likely be even more severe and difficult to overcome. The test forces you to stand your ground and believe in what your gut is telling you even though you have no guarantee that you are right, no encouraging signs, and no idea how it will all work out. The only thing you have is a wobbly inner knowing.

What we could not know when making our election day choice, or while enduring the ensuing test in that first year after the election, was that taking shape in the background long before the election ever took place, a group who cared deeply about what was happening in our country and our world was conducting careful study, quiet research, and meticulous preparation. They were planning to end the corruption, take down the Globalists, and end their corrupt New World Order. Someone was about to stand up and say something.

In early November 2017, I was browsing through YouTube channels when I happened across a title that struck me as odd: *Massive Intel Drop Q Clearance 4Chan – Part 2.*[32] I don't know why this interested me, but it did. I clicked on it and entered a world of intrigue. The guy presenting these cryptic messages, James Munder, started off with the casual remark that he was high on coke but had to comment on these Q drops.

"High on coke?" I thought. "How real can this be?" Still, after listening, I had to check it out, so I went to the 4Chan site to look around. I got in, but it was difficult to navigate. Posts on the 4Chan board were brutally direct, full of words I'd never heard, and laced with obscenities. I went back to the relative calm of YouTube and went looking for more information on Q.[33] Eventually, I learned that someone with a Q-level clearance is someone who has access to top secret information. Whoever Q was, he (or she, or they) had recently written the following:

> My fellow Americans, over the course of the next several days you will undoubtedly realize that we are taking back our great country (the land of the free) from the evil tyrants that

32 Munder, James. *Massive Intel Drop Q Clearance 4Chan-Pt. 2.* 9 November 2017. https://www.youtube.com/watch?v=wpKA9xMgWkU.

33 Munder, James. *Massive Intel Drop Q Clearance 4Chan-Pt. 1.* 9 November 2017https://www.youtube.com/watch?v=1yP3-NqAao0.

wish to do us harm and destroy the last remaining refuge of shining light. On POTUS' order, we have initiated certain fail-safes that shall safeguard the public from the primary fallout which is slated to occur 11.3 upon the arrest announcement of Mr. Podesta (actionable 11.4).

Confirmation (to the public) of what is occurring will then be revealed and will not be openly accepted. Public riots are being organized in serious numbers in an effort to prevent the arrest and capture of more senior public officials. On POTUS' order, a state of temporary military control will be actioned and special ops carried out. False leaks have been made to retain several within the confines of the United States to prevent extradition and special operator necessity.

Rest assured, the safety and well-being of every man, woman, and child of this country is being exhausted in full. However, the atmosphere within the country will unfortunately be divided as so many have fallen for the corrupt and evil narrative that has long been broadcast. We will be initiating the Emergency Broadcast System (EMS) during this time in an effort to provide a direct message (avoiding the fake news) to all citizens.

Organizations and/or people that wish to do us harm during this time will be met with swift fury—certain laws have been pre-lifted to provide our great military the necessary authority to handle and conduct these operations (at home and abroad).

Another post continued:

POTUS will be well insulated/protected on AF1 and abroad (specific locations classified) while these operations are conducted due to the nature of the entrenchment. It is time to take back our country and make America great again. Let us salute and pray for the brave men and women in uniform who will undertake this assignment to bring forth peace, unity, and return power to the people.

It is our hope that this message reaches enough people to make a meaningful impact. We cannot yet telegraph this message through normal methods for reasons I'm sure everyone here can understand. Follow the questions from the previous thread(s) and remain calm, the primary targets are within DC and remain at the top (on both sides). The spill over in the streets will be quickly shut down. Look for more false flags—stay alert, be vigilant, and above all, please pray.

For God so loved the world that he gave his one and only son, that whoever believes in him shall not perish but have eternal life. Love is patient, love is kind."

God bless my fellow Americans.

4, 10, 20

These posts were followed by this:

(4Chan) Bread Crumbs – Q Clearance Patriot (10/31/2017 (Tue) 20:00:15)

There are more good people than bad. The wizards and warlocks (inside term) will not allow another Satanic Evil POS to control our country. Realize Soros, Clintons, Obama, Putin, etc., are all controlled by three families (the 4th was removed post Trump's victory).

11.3 – Podesta indicted

11.6 – Huma indicted

Manafort was placed into Trump's camp (as well as others). The corruption that will come out is so serious that deals must be cut for people to walk away, otherwise 70% of elected politicians would be in jail (you are seeing it already begin). A deep cleaning is occurring and the prevention and defense of pure evil is occurring on a daily basis. They never thought they were going to lose control of the Presidency (not just D's) and thought they had control since making past mistakes (JFK, Reagan).

God speed, Patriots.

PS, Soros is targeted.

Digging a little further, I found a QAnon post from Saturday, November 4, 2017 that focused on Saudi Arabia:

By the time POTUS returns from his trip the world will be a different place.
Godfather III
Alice & Wonderland
Alice (Lewis Carroll) =
The Bloody Wonderland =
(Repost)
Why did JK[34] travel to SA recently?
What is SA known for?
Where do the biggest donations originate from?
Why is this relevant?
What else is relevant w/SA?
Safe harbor?
Port of transfer?
Why was there a recent smear campaign against JK and POTUS?
Why is the timing important?

(2nd Post [Repost Lost])
Martial law declared in SA.
Why is this relevant?
How much money was donated to CF by SA?
How much money was donated to John M Institute by SA?
How much money was donated to Pelosi Foundation?
How much money was donated to CS by SA?

---

34 JK = Jared Kushner, SA = Saudi Arabia, CF = Clinton Foundation, John M Institute = John McCain Institute, CS = Chuck Schumer, NG = National Guard, BO = Barack Obama, NK = North Korea, D = Democrat, HUMA = Harvard University Muslim Alumni, MB = Muslim Brotherhood, HRC = Hillary Rodham Clinton.

What other bad actors have been paid by SA (bribed) (Not just D's)?

Why did the Bush family recently come out against POTUS?

Who is good?

What are the laws in SA v. US (charged criminals)?

What information might be gained by these detainees?

Why is this important?

SA → US

What force is actively deployed in SA?

NG?

Have faith.

These, the crumbs, in time, will equate to the biggest drops ever disclosed in our history.

Remember, disinformation is real.

God bless.

Alice & Wonderland

The Great Awakening.

Q

After reading the QAnon posts, I realized that the arrests of over 20 powerful men from the royal family in Saudi Arabia was more significant than I at first thought. I wondered what was going on over there, but little was said in mainstream news because people in America were still distracted by the mass shootings in Las Vegas and the church in Sutherland Springs, Texas.

I took the time to follow up on the Texas shooting, and when I heard that the kind of gun used to take out shooter Devin Kelley was the same kind of gun Kelley was using to shoot up the church, I knew in my gut that this mass shooting was a turning point in the argument to institute gun control and take away our guns. They would lose. The fact that Stephen Willeford was a simple, god-fearing man who trained people how to use guns responsibly, that he had exactly the same automatic rifle in his gun closet that was the subject of so much controversy, that he knew how to use it well, and he was brave enough to go after the gunman shooting in the church, was something that the Cabal could not have prepared for.

I took it as a sign. Either the Cabal was getting sloppy, or the tides were turning against them, or their old trick of creating a mass shooting to distract people from events that might cause them to probe deeper was not working.

A post from November 5 was:

> Follow HUMA.
> Who connects HRC/CF to SA?
> Why is this relevant
> Who is the Muslim Brotherhood?
> Who has ties to the MB?
> Who is Awan?
> What is the Awan Group?
> Where do they have offices?
> Why is this relevant?
> Define cash laundering.
> What is the relationship between SA & Pakistan?
> Why is this relevant?
> Why would SA provide tens of millions of dollars to US senior govt. officials?
> What does SA obtain in exchange for payment?
> Why is access important?
> What happened when HRC lost the election of 2016?
> How much money was provided to the CF by SA during 15/16?
> HRC lost.
> Loss of access/power/control.
> Does repayment of funds to SA occur? If so, how?
> Why did BO send billions in cash to Iran?
> Why wasn't Congress notified?
> Why was this classified under State Secrets?
> Who has access to State Secrets?
> Where did the planes carrying the cash depart from and land?
> Did the planes all land in the same location?
> How many planes carried the cash?
> Why is this relevant? What does this have to do w/NK?
> What does this have to do w/SA/CF cash donations?
> What does this have to do w/ISIS?

What does this have to do w/slush funds?
Why is SA so vitally important?
Follow the money.
Who has the money?
What is happening in SA today?
Why is this relevant?
Who was Abdullah bin Abdulaziz?
What events transpired directly thereafter?
How was POTUS greeted compared to other US. presidents
when in SA?
Why is this relevant?
What is the meaning of this tradition?
What coincidentally was the last Tweet sent out by POTUS?
Why is this relevant?
Where was POTUS when that Tweet was sent?
Why is that relevant?
What attack took place in SA as operations were undertaken?
Flying objects.
What US operators are currently in SA?
Why is this relevant?
Questions provide answers.
Alice & Wonderland.

What was going on? Could it be happening? Was someone standing up and saying something? Were they going after the corruption in our government? I could hardly sleep that night.

I began to hang out on YouTube daily, something I'd never done before, always in search of the latest information from Q or info that might clarify the messages from Q since they were all dropped in the form of cryptic questions and abbreviations.[35] I learned that it was illegal to leak classified information in the form of statements that directly express what

---

35 For an introduction to the Q material, see *Q For Beginners, Part 1* and *Part 2*. https://www.youtube.com/watch?v=ymIENvtcJqo/.

was happening, but it was not illegal to leak information in the form of questions.

Q referred to his questions as *crumbs* and urged us to gather the crumbs then *bake bread*, a euphemism for putting together something that would feed us a more complete picture of what was happening. He would drop a hint about what was going to happen, then say, "Future proves past," and within a few days or weeks, the event or story he foretold would occur, demonstrating that he was not only right, he was in touch with the President and had the highest level of information.

There were not just questions to answer, there were strings of numbers and sets of initials to be deciphered, odd references to Alice *&* Wonderland instead of Alice *In* Wonderland, and unusual directions such as *follow the White Rabbit*.[36] All of this forced those of us following Q to think for ourselves, sent us scrambling for additional information, and brought together an entire network of people who kept sharing their thoughts, perceptions, and the possible decoded answers that came out of the research. I began to understand that the reason the information was being dropped on the 4Chan and 8Chan political boards was because the people who frequented that site could see through the smoke and mirrors of the Cabal, questioned everything the mainstream news presented, were keenly critical of doublespeak, and were willing to call a spade a spade. These were computer geeks who referred to themselves as *autists*[37] and had no intention of apologizing for the fact that they were nerds whose passion was truth regarding reality and all things computer. ✌

---

36 It turned out much later that a person who traffics children for purposes of supplying others with child sex is called a *white rabbit*.

37 "Autist" is the nickname given to those on 4Chan and 8Chan who decoded the Q drops and did much of the research to flesh out Q's information.

7 ✃

The Sting

As November and December passed, I continued to track every message, reading them again and again, trying to understand the crumbs and piece together a bigger picture of what was happening, as well as what was coming toward us. A rough outline of what was taking place began taking shape, and although the picture had many holes and lots of questions, I realized a massive sting was taking place, courtesy of Donald Trump, the military, and the Q team.

From that point on, a story began to emerge that was like watching an Agatha Christie mystery unfold in real time right in front of my nose! A few good men who loved us, our country, our way of life, and our constitution had been watching what was happening in our country at least since the September 11 attacks. Originally, they planned to carry out a full-scale coup d'état to take back our country from those who intended to collapse all nations in order to create the New World Order. Their coup plans changed after that initial meeting in Monaco hosted by Neil Keenan in 2012.

These men had access to great power, but they knew power was not enough. The Cabal had control of all media in the U.S. and no coup had a chance of succeeding without control of the media.

When Obama renewed the National Defense Authorization Act (NDAA) in 2013, it contained the legal right for new media to pump out propaganda instead of news. Since propaganda is the propagation of "ideas or statements that are often false or exaggerated and that are spread in order to help a government,"[35] it was easy to control our perception and what the masses believed. In addition to propaganda, the media had the option of choosing which stories to bury so the public was never informed about what was really happening.

With these facts in mind, the group planning the takeover knew that a coup in America could be quickly put down and would be reported as little more than a scuffle in the barnyard, easily ended by locking the barnyard gates and engaging in a corral shoot, if needed. The whole scuffle could be blamed on North Korea, ISIS, Arabs with boxcutters, or whomever because the American people were still asleep and would believe whatever they were told.

The Cabal was deeply embedded in every nation on the planet. They had weapons that were capable of mass destruction. They had secret communication satellites in orbit courtesy of Elon Musk and SpaceX.[36] They had many people on their side who were in positions of great power controlling banking, trade, commodities, academia, and energy.

----

35 Dykes, Melissa. *Yes, US Government Propaganda Use Against American Citizens is Officially Legal Now*. Activist Post. 18 August 2016. https://www.activistpost.com/2016/08/yes-us-government-propaganda-use-american-citizens-officially-legal-now.html

36 "In November of 2018, the United States Federal Communications Commission (FCC) authorised the rocket company SpaceX, owned by the entrepreneur Elon Musk, to launch a fleet of 7,518 satellites to complete SpaceX's ambitious scheme to provide global satellite broadband services to every corner of the Earth. The satellites will operate at a height of approximately 210 miles, and irradiate the Earth with extremely high frequencies between 37.5 GHz and 42 GHz. This fleet will be in addition to a smaller SpaceX fleet of 4,425 satellites, already authorised earlier in the year by the FCC, which will orbit the Earth at a height of approximately 750 miles and is set to bathe us in frequencies between 12 GHz and 30 GHz. The grand total of SpaceX satellites is thus projected to reach just under 12,000." Children's Health Defense on Collective Evolution. 26 April 2019. https://www.collective-evolution.com/2019/04/26/5g-from-space-not-one-inch-of-the-globe-will-be-free-of-radiation/.

The American people were being kept in the dark, and my clients in other countries would often ask me point blank, "What is going *on* over there!!?? Why are you people allowing yourselves to be destroyed?" The answer was simple. Americans didn't have a clue what was really happening in our country. None of the mainstream news outlets were telling us real news, and what little information was being handed out was carefully slanted and presented to make us think what the Cabal wanted us to think and to see the world the way they wanted us to see it. We were being manipulated six ways to Sunday. People outside the country could see it, but we couldn't.

❧

Eventually, those planning to stand up and say something in the form of a coup realized that what they needed was people's understanding, support, and their hearts. Otherwise, a military coup could create a huge backlash and all could be lost. Besides, it was against the very constitution they were trying to save. In the end, the coup idea was scrapped and they decided to develop a more comprehensive plan, one that was more likely to succeed.

They began looking for someone who could be president that had a similar love of country and constitution, was ethical, smart, worldly, and tough. They needed a president who would cooperate with them, allowing them to use the tools at their disposal to end the corruption, while the president used his own tools and skills to rebuild America. Their common goal was to take down the devious men and women guilty of high treason, fraud, money laundering, sex trafficking, organ trafficking, drug trafficking, pedophilia, and child sacrifice.

It isn't clear how they settled on Donald Trump. It might have been the fact that he was a member of the elites and knew what was going on in that world. Maybe it was because he had run for president in the past. Perhaps it was his extensive dealings and connections around the world, or maybe that he had been the best friend of John F. Kennedy, Jr. and was outraged by JFK Jr.'s untimely and highly suspicious death that cleared the path for Hillary Clinton to run for the U.S. Senate representing New York.

Whatever it was that made Trump stand out to these military planners, they recruited him with promises that they would make sure the voting machines were not rigged so it would be an honest election, and they would protect him and his family completely.

Whether or not the original planners knew what they were getting into when they asked Trump to join the team, I'm sure they were surprised after he joined them. An important aspect of Trump is that he is instinctively strategic and everything he says or does is a very calculated move. I have heard a number of people remark that "nothing sticks to Trump." I read somewhere that the reason challenges roll off his back is because *whatever reaction is coming at him is exactly what he was trying to create, which only confirms that he is in control of the situation.*

In many ways, Trump was the perfect addition to the military team. Under the umbrella of their collective mindset, the plan changed from a military coup in America to take-down of the Cabal, return of sovereignty to the people, and a sea-change in leadership and planetary direction.

This required a more comprehensive plan, something with more finesse. Every single possible play and potential outcome was explored down to the smallest detail. Every strategy was mapped out, played out in their minds, acted out among them as they explored approaches and responses until every angle had been examined and every tool, skill, or asset that might be needed was assembled and made ready. They worked out Trump's campaign strategy, how he would use Twitter to go directly to the people and bypass the corrupt media's biased reporting, distortions, and misrepresentations. They covered how Trump would act and what he would say in his first year, who he would appoint into various positions and how long they would stay. They decided which members of the Cabal would be given positions of power in order to carefully surveil and track them to see who they were secretly communicating with and where the payoffs were going. The hope was to smoke out the big players at the top while the daily public theater distracted from their hidden action. Trump would hold the fort in the White House while the military was working quietly but powerfully in the background, dealing with the corruption itself.

Once Trump was elected and inaugurated, he and the military group working with him allowed things to meander slowly forward. The Trump team wanted their opponents to think that Trump was somewhat disorganized and nothing was happening that was any different from the startup of any other presidential term.

While the mainstream media hacked away at the new president as having been sexually inappropriate, or reported that the administration was chaotic and inept, Hillary Clinton and the Democratic National Committee insisted there was collusion between Trump and the Russians to influence the election. They kept pushing for an investigation with the intent of challenging the legitimacy of the president's election to office.

In retaliation, Trump fired FBI Director James Comey, saying Comey had mishandled the investigation into Hillary's use of a private email server. This firing triggered a call for a Special Counsel to investigate Trump, leading Department of Justice Deputy Attorney General Rod Rosenstein to appoint Robert Mueller. Meanwhile, the media continued to attack, blaming Trump for everything under the sun.

As the new administration got itself organized, Trump put people into positions of power that he and the Q team knew were connected to the corruption. This allowed the team to watch them even more closely, listen in to all their communications, and gather direct evidence of who was engaged in corruption, how much of it, and where the money was going.

For those of us reading the news and listening to mainstream media, it seemed to me and others I talked with that Trump appeared to be unable to fight back effectively. We never suspected that this was a deliberate act. Those who elected him continued to wring their hands anxiously and suffer the onslaughts of the media that NEVER said anything positive about him. Anyone who tried to say anything about the corruption that was going on was accused of being a conspiracy nut. Often, those same accusations were turned around and directed at the Trump team. At times, it looked like nothing was getting done. Trump continued to fire his own appointees and was back-pedaling a lot.

However, the whole thing was a ruse, the setup for a massive sting. Corrupt Democrats, rotten Republicans, mainstream media colluders, traitors in the FBI, the CIA, Department of Justice and others—all played right into Trump's hands.

In early October 2017, nearly a year after the election, Trump and team were ready. He gathered the team and their wives together for dinner and a group photograph. It was during the photo session that he made the remark that this was "the calm before the storm." When reporters and photographers asked what he meant by that, he replied, "You'll see."

It was later that same month, almost the end of October, that QAnon began posting his intelligence drops, revealing that the takedown of the corruption was about to begin with operations planned in Saudi Arabia first, then the U.S., then Asia, and finally Europe.

⚙

It isn't known exactly when Trump began meeting with the Saudi regime or what he said to them, but he made an official visit to Saudi Arabia in May of 2017. This was only 3½ months after he became president. When he arrived, the Saudis honored him with a traditional sword dance and described his visit as "a reset of the regional order."[37] There were some talks, some deals worth billions, and, to those of us watching, it appeared that Trump went quietly on his way. There was no hint of what was to come.

The next time we heard about Saudi Arabia was on the first weekend in November of 2017 when Crown Prince Mohammed bin Salman arrested dozens of Saudis said to be involved in serious corruption activities. Among those arrested was Prince Alwaleed bin Talal,[38] the powerful and corrupt man who funded Barack Obama's education and groomed him for a political career as president of the United States.

---

37 Chulov, Martin. *Saudi Leaders Hail Trump Visit as 'Reset of Regional Order.'* The Guardian. 20 May 2017. https://www.theguardian.com/us-news/2017/may/20/trump-visit-hailed-by-saudi-leaders-as-reset-of-regional-order

38 This page has since been removed from the internet. http://digg.com/2017/saudi-arabia-princes-arrested-corruption-salman-talal

What we *didn't* hear and *didn't* know was that a month earlier, Trump and Saudi officials were to meet in Las Vegas on the top floors of the Mandalay Bay hotel. The top five floors are owned by Saudi Prince Alwaleed bin Talal,[39] and President Trump was there to have a secret meeting that night as he worked to bring about Saudi cooperation to end human trafficking and cut the streams of money coming in to pay-off American politicians for their cooperation in the September 11th attacks and other favors.[40]

Someone who was to be part of that secret meeting must have leaked the details to the Cabal and a plan was put in place to assassinate Trump. MS13 gang members were posing as security guards to back up the CIA assassins who were to carry out the plan. However, something went wrong. A gunfight ensued, perhaps before Trump ever got off his plane, which had landed at McCarran Airport right next to a music festival. It appears that foolish, last-ditch efforts were made to use high-powered automatic weapons to shoot Trump's plane, but only ended up going as far as the festival. Music coming from the festival made enough noise at first to cover the sound of guns. People in nearby hotels thought that firecrackers were going off at the festival, a fact that added to the confusion at the scene. I read somewhere that the Las Vegas massacre was originally planned to be much larger—on the scale of the September 11 disaster—but I could not find that reference and had to be content with being happy that things don't always go as planned.

No one was expecting it when, only a month after the Las Vegas massacre, the Saudi Arabian crown prince carried out arrests of those involved in corrupt child sex-trafficking rings operating in his country. Twenty Saudi princes and a host of government ministers, members of the Saudi military, and businessmen were arrested and their assets frozen then confiscated in a massive crackdown on the corruption.

---

39 Jeter, Robert. *Saudi Prince Alwaleed bin Talal: Las Vegas Conspiracy Grows*. The Trump Times. 7 November 2017. https://thetrumptimes. com/2017/11/07/saudi-prince-alwaleed-bin-talal-las-vegas-conspiracy-grows/

40 www.qmap.pub. Drop #92, *Las Vegas Mass Shooting*. 5 Nov 2017. Drop #117, *Saudi Prince Alwaleed Arrest*, 6 Nov 2017. Drop #154, *Who Financed 9-11*, 14 Nov 2017.

Saudi Arabia was the centerpiece whose funding backed underage sex trafficking, money laundering, and other unsavory operations. The Saudis also funded the Clintons and regularly sent money to the Clinton Foundation to buy influence and access to power in the U.S.

It is likely U.S. Marines, Navy Seals, and/or the National Guard assisted in the Saudi arrests that not only cut the flow of secret money into U.S. political pockets, but also cut off as many human trafficking lanes around the world as possible, including the trafficking being carried on by the Red Cross and the Clinton Foundation. The Clinton Foundation was smuggling children out of Haiti, and the Red Cross was smuggling everything everywhere.[41] [42]

The Saudi operation was a red flag of warning for those involved in the corruption around the world. In December 2017, Q post #392 announced that, so far, more than 3,000 children had been rescued in Saudi Arabia alone.

Much later, one of the 8Chan autists who complained about how long it was taking to settle things wrote, "I hope Q understands that, while we are standing firm, many of us are losing family and friends. I believe it is worth it. I hope to God it's worth it. I know I've paid a heavy price for my loyalty."

Q's reply in Drop #1964 was brutally blunt in response. "Patriot, a little perspective…children are being kidnapped, tortured, raped, and sacrificed in the name of PURE EVIL. Stay the course. We are fighting a deeply entrenched enemy."

Then things began to happen quickly in the U.S. Tony Podesta, owner of one of the biggest lobbying firms in Washington, D.C., and the

---

41 Report of the International Federation. *Human Trafficking and Smuggling*. 7 June 2004. https://www.ifrc.org/en/news-and-media/opinions-and-positions/speeches/2004/human-trafficking-and-smuggling/

42 www.qmap.pub. See drop #258, *Red Cross Stringer*; 4 Dec 2017. Drop #392, *3000+ Children Saved*; 19 Dec 2017. Drop #489, *US Taxpayers Funding the Scams*; 7 Jan 2018. Drop #1249, *Red Cross Smuggling What?* 23 Apr 2018.

brother of John Podesta, suddenly closed his lobbying business and let all of his employees go with a mere two weeks notice.

Huma Abedin, wife of former Congressman Anthony Weiner and long-time personal assistant to Hillary Clinton, suddenly dropped out of sight. Hillary Clinton, John McCain, and a couple of others began wearing unlikely surgical boots and claiming they'd had foot trouble. Hillary said it was a broken toe, something that takes 4-6 weeks to heal. More than two months later she was still wearing the boot. McCain's story was that he'd had surgery on his Achilles heel, but a week or so later he forgot which leg he had been putting the boot on, and he put it on the wrong leg. Even Chelsea Clinton was seen wearing a boot. When Hillary's boot finally came off, the outline of a device encircling her ankle was clearly visible under her pant leg. The speculation was that they were all wearing geo-location devices that prevented them from leaving the country or going into hiding.

There were many arrests in several countries, as well as unusual power outages at airports. Airplane flights were forced to turn around[43] or be shot down because someone was trying to flee the country. There was also a noticeable increase in the number of flights going back and forth to Guantanamo Bay Prison in Cuba, suggesting that a number of unknown people were being taken to Gitmo.

There was the crash of a helicopter killing several people who were witnesses to sex trafficking at the hotel they managed, an attempt to derail a train full of Republican congressmen and their families by using a garbage truck, and many other events hardly given a mention by mainstream media.

Almost from the start, QAnon began directing attention to the various foundations operated by Clinton, McCain, Pelosi, and others. He pointed out that these foundations were not used to do good or make the world a better place. They were used as slush funds for bribery, wetworks (murder), or other unsavory obligations that paid people to engage in illegal activities, vote as told, or be silent and look the other way when they

---

43 www.qmap.pub. Drop #67 *TSA and Airplanes*; 3 Nov 2017.

saw something that should not be happening. Included in the list were the Consumer Protection Agency and several environmental organizations.

The McCain Institute,[44] supposedly formed to fight human trafficking, took in money from donors like the Rothschilds, Saudi Arabia, and even accepted money from McCain's election campaign. However, each year it wrote only a single check. It was to Arizona State University Foundation, which has nothing to do with human trafficking. In 2012 and 2013, the check to ASU was for $500,000. In 2014, it went up to $1.5 million. What did ASU do with that money? Was ASU Foundation part of a money laundering operation? What did the McCain Institute do with the rest of the money they took in? In addition to exposing some foundations as fronts, Q alerted people to several coming false flags as well as a number of connections between events that we would never have known because mainstream media was not doing its job at all.

When the FBI Deputy Director Andrew McCabe and Associate Deputy Attorney General Bruce Ohr did not show up to testify at their respective hearings before the Senate Intelligence Committee regarding what each knew about the Fusion GPS dossier, it was clear the gloves were coming off. Those involved in the corruption were being forced into a corner, forced to take a stand. When members of the FBI ignore the workings of due process and our system of laws, they are broadcasting their allegiance to another ruler or system and basically saying *you're not the boss of me*. "Who are they aligned with?" I worried. "Who are they listening to? These are smart, powerful men. They wouldn't be acting like this if they didn't think the group they were aligned with was going to

---

44 This page was available on 2 June 2019 and was removed suddenly by 8 June 2019 after I made several visits to it. https://thecyrusreport.blogspot.com/2017/02/mccain-foundation-nothing-more-than.html.

Burns, Jack. *Follow the Money: Senator John McCain's Ties to Saudis and Rothschilds EXPOSED*. The Free Thought Project. 8 March 2017. https://thefreethoughtproject.com/john-mccains-connections-human-rights-abusers-wealthy-elitists/ (visited last on June 2, 2019).

Dmitry, Baxter. *McCain Institute Caught Stealing Millions in Child Trafficking Donations*. News Punch. 25 February 2017. https://newspunch.com/mccain-institute-child-trafficking/ (last visited June 2, 2019).

win and they would be safe. Whoever it is has to be at least as big, well-established and organized as the United States legal system."

It was not until much later that I realized McCabe and Ohr were refusing to break rank in the futile hope that they would prevail. They probably also feared being murdered if they showed signs of weakening or of becoming a potential informant against others in the Cabal.

While Saudi Arabia was arresting the leaders of corruption in Saudi Arabia, U.S. politicians, CEOs, and academics involved in human trafficking, pedophilia, and kickbacks were being confronted with audio, video, and financial evidence of their corruption and given a choice—either drop out of politics, step down from their positions of power, or be charged publicly with their crimes and go to jail. The result was a record number of sudden resignations by people who were at the top of their game or long-time pillars of government. Some of the most visible and surprising were Paul Ryan, Cory Booker, John Conyers, and Lamar Alexander. As mentioned earlier, according to Q, 70% of Washington, D.C. was involved in corrupt activity and it was necessary to make deals with many of them or the entire government would have collapsed. To date, there have been over 7,000 inexplicable resignations from prominent positions around the world.[45] [46] Granted, some of the more recent resignations could be unrelated to the corruption, but most of those occurring in late 2017 and through 2018 were related to the Trump sting.

In addition to resignations, Trump and the Q team began working to cut off income streams that were keeping the Cabal operatives alive. Shortly after the takedown of the Cabal began, the opium processing plants built in Afghanistan were bombed out of existence, severely cutting

---

45 DeSilver, Drew. *Near-record Number of House Members Not Seeking Re-election in 2018*. Pew Research Center. 11 April 2018. https://www. pewresearch.org/fact-tank/2018/04/11/near-record-number-of-house-members-not-seeking-re-election-in-2018/

46 List of resignations. https://www.qmap.pub/resignations

into their pockets.[47] The mainstream media spun this into a story that we were bombing the Taliban, but the truth was that the Taliban, like ISIS and al Qaeda, were being supported by the Cabal—and used by them as well.

Income streams going into the Clinton Foundation, the McCain Institute, the Pelosi Foundation, and other programs were also cut because these funds were being used personally and for numerous other illegal purposes.[48]

I felt a weird combination of relief and sadness as I watched congressmen and CEOs step down and announce they would not be returning after Christmas break or would not be running for office again. Those who stepped down were warned that good people would be watching their activities, but I wondered, "How long will this last unless *we, the American people, begin watching and paying attention?*" &

---

47 Kube, Courtney; Nichols, Hans; Gains, Mosheh. *U.S. on Track to Triple Bombs Dropped on Afghanistan Against Taliban.* CBS News; source Reuters. 20 November 2017. https://www.nbcnews.com/news/world/u-s-bombs-afghan-opium-plants-new-strategy-cut-taliban-n822506

48 www.qmap.pub. Drop #53, *Corrupt Foundations and IRS*; 2 Nov 2017. Drop #1825, *MSM $160MM Slush Fund to Counter Conservatives*; 7 August 2018. Drop #779, *Senator Warren & Consumer Protection Agency Corruption*; 15 February 2018. Drop #1179, *Scott Pruitt Has the Goods on EPA Slush Funds*; 19 April 2018. Drop #5, *Follow the Money, It's the Key*; 29 October 2017.

8 ❧

A Look Behind the Curtain

FROM THE MOMENT I DISCOVERED THE QANON DROPS I BECAME FASCINATED by what was going on behind the curtain on the Washington stage. In a couple of early posts (#133 & #140), Q outlined the structure of power running the world.[52] The symbol of this power is the familiar pyramid with the all-seeing eye in it. The pyramid has three sides with each side representing a specific family group. The family groups represented by these three sides are the House of Saud worth $4 trillion, the Rothschilds worth $2 trillion, and the Soros group worth $1 trillion. These three families make up the triangle that forms the New World Order. (NWO [53])

Although the House of Saud has more money, the Rothschilds are the NWO cult leaders.[54] Each family group handles a specific kind of business. The Rothschild group handles money, banking, and all things financial. They control governments and most, but not all, politicians. They manage the flesh markets, trigger recurring financial fiascoes that threaten the entire western banking system, create recessions, and collapse

---

52 www.qmap,pub. Drop #133 *The Puppetmasters;* 11 Nov 2017. Drop #140 *Families Combined (TRI) = NWO*. 11 Nov 2017.

53 Although this is often said to mean "New World Order", it actually means "Naturaliche Wirtschaftordnung" which translates to "Natural Economic Order."

54 www.qmap.pub. Drop #299 *Rothschilds Cult Leaders*; 7 Dec 2017.

a US bank or two on occasion. They print counterfeit U.S. dollars by the truckload and use these to bribe people to go along with NWO plans and programs. They will also hand out trillions of dollars to themselves while declaring they are saving the financial system.

The House of Saud handles energy, oil, and the technology sectors, as well as the sex trade involving children. Although their specialty is energy and oil, Saudi Arabia was specifically assigned to manage and control U.S. and U.K. politicians, along with the big technology and media companies. This includes Facebook, Twitter, Reddit, NBC, MSNBC, ABC, CBS, CNN, Fox News, and the Washington Post. Saudi Arabia was the port of call for thousands of children being traded or used as pay-offs around the world. These children were generally used for sex, for hunting, and for ritual sacrifice, although some were used in adrenochrome operations. Reports among the Q posts indicated that as many as 3,000 children were kept on hand at all times in Saudi Arabia, with blond, blue-eyed children fetching premium prices. Sadly, anyone with a twisted mind would gravitate to these types of Saudi dealings, looking for acceptance and inclusion in something that would sanction their twisted approach to children.

The Soros group handles all things related to population and the mass manipulation of people. They fund hundreds of socialist and subversive groups in almost every country around the world. MoveOn.org is an example here. The Soros arm handles brainwashing organizations, the management of slush funds, the movement of large groups of people, and a variety of decisions and pacts that involve consumers and the environment. Soros operatives herded millions of refugees from the Middle East into Europe, collapsing European cultures and forcing nations into chaos, while hoping to eventually collapse borders and make it easier to implement the New World Order. Soros and the entire NWO are experts at using Naomi Wolf's Shock Doctrine on a global scale—create a problem, then offer the solution that contains the change you wanted to make. This, in fact, is the whole foundation of terrorism.

I have long felt that the NWO used two things to lure people into their traps. Of course, one was copious amounts of money. The other was their ability to convince people that there was no way they could lose. The idea of unlimited money and power would be quite convincing, and the willingness to murder anyone who got in the way would be quite effective. Thinking that the side you are on is invincible would be very attractive to those oriented to power over others.

The families forming the three sides of the NWO triangle are based on bloodlines that are carefully tracked, and all of them worship Satan, a fact they are trying to legitimize and normalize within our culture. Q called these three families the *Puppetmasters.* They are the ones who were pulling the strings of power around the world until Donald Trump cut many of those strings,[55] especially the payments made to coerce U.S. politicians into making decisions that ignored the will of the people and instead favored corporate and foreign interests.

An example of the way the things work in reality can be seen in the events of September 11th. When the House of Saud, specialists in energy and oil, began running low on oil and needed more productive oil wells, they financed the September 11th attacks. The U.S. made up the story that Iraq had perpetrated the attacks and then proceeded to invade Iraq and take control of their oil wells, which were then handed over to Saudi Arabia to manage and profit from. What did the U.S. get out of this? They got continued support for the U.S. dollar as the world's reserve currency.

The September 11th attack also helped the Cabal begin the process of gutting the U.S. Constitution via the Patriot Act, which was prepared long before the attacks took place. Conveniently, the attack also destroyed the investigations being conducted by the Navy into massive financial irregularities. One investigation was being run and accumulating evidence in the exact offices that were destroyed in the Pentagon. The other investigation was being run and evidence collected in Building 7 in New York, which collapsed out of the blue, late in the day on September 11th.

---

55 www.qmap.pub. Drop #99 *Strings Cut in Saudi Arabia.* 5 Nov 2017.

Fairly early in the intelligence drops by Q, he outlined *The 16-Year Plan.*[56] This plan allotted eight years to Barack Obama and another eight to Hillary Clinton to accomplish certain tasks that would complete the takeover by the New World Order. From the point of view of the Cabal, it was time to push their agenda at top speed before anyone was the wiser. Their hurry was sparked by their biggest fear—that the American people were waking up and would soon realize what was happening.

During Barack's time, he was to install rogue operators in many of the top positions within government. He would also cut funding to the military and leak classified intelligence about military assets. This would allow potential enemies to plan and build weaponry to counter us very effectively. He would take command away from the generals by insisting they call the White House and get permission to run any kind of attack or operation, which would then give the White House time to warn members of Al Qaeda or ISIS that an attack was coming, giving them time to prepare or move people and equipment out of the way.

Under Obama's watch, Special Access Programs would be for sale, and Prism and Keyscore software would become open source, which would cripple the U.S. military. He was to target and weaken the conservative base in the U.S. by harassing them through the IRS and mainstream media, open the borders to flood the country with illegals who would vote democratic, and continue funding ISIS and MS13 groups as domestic assets to be used within the U.S. as needed.

He would turn a blind eye to Iran and North Korea in their building of nuclear weapons, overlook the sale of uranium that would eventually go to Iran and North Korea, and would kill NASA in order to prevent space domination by the U.S. This would also result in the takedown of military satellites, leave us helpless in the face of an EMP from space, and allow the Cabal to install weapons of mass destruction based in space.

During Hillary's eight years, she was to complete our takedown. She was tasked with starting WWIII. This was going to be a fake war that

---

56 www.qmap.pub. Drop #570 *The 16 Year Plan to Destroy America.* 21 Jan 2018.

would be talked up in the mainstream news, but without any real conflicts between countries. People would see that others were dying, killed in attacks as reported by the news media, but the real reason they were dying was the secret use of weapons of mass destruction. Eventually, it would be announced that the U.S. had lost the war and was a conquered nation.

Hillary was tasked with getting rid of the remaining government and military operators who were loyal to the former structure of the U.S. She would take down the economy, open the borders even further, revise the Constitution, and ban firearms by taking out the Second Amendment.

In addition, the Supreme Court was to be loaded with liberals who would rule against any challenges to her authority, and the Electoral College was to be removed, making manipulation of voting much easier with the use of Soros-owned voting machines. Hillary would eliminate any remaining funding for the U.S. military, close all U.S. military bases around the world, and destroy alternative news sources while censoring everything else. She would oversee the republishing of facts and would keep distractions high. The secret motto for her presidency was to be, "Keep them starved. Keep them blind. Keep them stupid."

For many years, the Cabal plan was working. Between 2009 and 2013, a serious amount of money began flowing into the Clinton Foundation. It came from a handful of people who wanted Hillary Clinton to approve the sale of a Canadian uranium mining company to a Russian mining company. The Canadian company held rights to mine uranium in the U.S. Since uranium is considered to be a very strategic asset, the sale of the company to a Russian mining entity had to be approved by the U.S. government, including, and especially, the State Department. Hillary Clinton was the Secretary of State, and she signed off on the deal knowing full well that this would give Russia control of 20% of our uranium.[57]

---

57 Rappaport, Jon. https://jonrappoport.wordpress.com/2016/01/27/the-clintons-is-the-oregon-standoff-really-about-uranium/
Also, do a search on Google under "clinton uranium Malheur connection"

Sitting on the land whose mineral and mining rights had just been sold to Russia was a 6,000-acre ranch owned by Dwight and Susan Hammond.[58] Dwight and his son Steve worked the ranch and raised cattle. For years, they were harassed by the Bureau of Land Management (BLM) and the Fish & Wildlife Service (FWS) who were secretly trying to get the Hammonds to sell the land and go elsewhere. The land was rich in an array of minerals from diamonds to uranium, gold, copper, and other metals, and the BLM and FWS wanted control over these riches.

The Hammond ranch was surrounded by the Malheur Wildlife Refuge. The Wildlife Refuge had originally been much smaller when it was first declared an Indian reservation (without Indians) back in 1908 by Theodore Roosevelt.[59] Since then, it had been systematically enlarged to 187,000 acres by the Fish & Wildlife Service.

To continue their underhanded enlargment of the refuge, the FWS would declare an area as a unique habitat for an *endangered* creature. In the case of the land around the Hammonds, this was the sage grouse. This declaration would severely limit what someone could do on their land.

In earlier days, many landowners around the Refuge had only small amounts of land and would then rent much larger tracts of pasture from the government. Little by little, hampered by steeply rising rental prices and an array of no-no's that always accompanied the declaration of a unique habitat, they would give up and go elsewhere, often selling whatever land they owned at a loss to the FWS, who would turn around and sell or lease the land at high prices to wealthy businessmen.

The Hammonds, who were unaware of the underlying scheme, had no idea what they were up against and kept hanging on. The Fish & Wildlife Service took them to court in an effort to take away their water

---

58 Ambellas, Shepard. 23 Jan 2016. https://www.intellihub.com/clinton-foundation-payoffs-promised-hammond-ranch-other-publically-owned-lands-russia/

59 Bundy, Clive. *Facts and Events in the Hammond Case.* Bundy Ranch Blogspot. 12 Nov 2015. http://bundyranch.blogspot.com/2015/11/facts-events-in-hammond-case.html

rights. The FWS lost, but then tried to build a fence around the Hammond's water. The Hammonds took it down.

Next, the ranch grazing permits were revoked. Following that, the Hammonds were told they had to build fences—miles of fences, forcing them to cut their ranch grazing land in half because fencing is expensive and requires a lot of work to maintain. Then the Bureau of Land Management closed and blocked the road that gave the Hammonds access to the upper part of their ranch. When the Hammonds drove around the blockade, they were threatened.

When Steve conducted a routine burn-off of grasses on their private land and it burned 127 acres of public land, the Hammonds put the fire out and no one thought anything about it because burning in order to refresh the land was a common practice. That was in the year 2001.

A host of other harrassments continued until, in 2006, a number of wildfires started by lightning were successfully stopped by Steve when he started a back fire. Unexpectedly, father and son were arrested for arson, and their homes were raided. Oddly, the case was never acted on until suddenly, in 2011 father and son were accused of being terrorists. They were arrested, convicted, fined $400,000 and sentenced to prison. Dwight served 3 months. Steve served 12 months. In 2015, they were re-sentenced (!) to another five years in prison by the infamous 9th District Court.

The Hammond's could not understand why they were being continuously harassed, and eventually their stubborn resistance to the tactics of the Bureau of Land Management and the Fish & Wildlife Service led to the standoff in Oregon in January 2016. The plight of the Hammonds had been monitored from a distance by the Clive Bundy family from Nevada who had just gone through the same kind of harassment. The Bundy land had been declared a habitat for the endangered desert turtle, but a standoff resulted in the backing down of the BLM and FWS.

When the Bundys heard what was happening to the Hammonds, they put out a call and were joined by a number of militiamen from around the U.S. who converged on the Malheur Wildlife Refuge and its small administration building. While occupying the building, they found papers indicating that the Russian mining company wanted to set up a large mining operation on the supposed wildlife refuge, and suddenly the whole picture was clear. The land was worth a fortune because it was loaded with uranium and precious metals. The BLM and FWS harassment had intensified because Hillary Clinton had approved the sale of the Canadian mining company holding rights to mine U.S. uranium to the Russian mining company that now wanted to come in and start digging. Belatedly, the Hammonds realized they were up against the entire U.S. government and a questionable, if not outright illegal, sale that the government wanted to cover up.

The Bundys and the Hammonds were targeted because they had valuable or strategic pieces of land. The men who made up the hidden militia in our United States joined them because they were recognizing a pattern that flew in the face of property rights in a republic. The BLM and other armed bureaucrats were then sent in to face down the armed militiamen and get the them, the Hammonds, and the Bundys to back down. The result was the stand-off that lasted for almost six weeks and resulted in one death that was deliberately set up by the government forces.

The standoff at the Bundy Ranch in Nevada and the Hammond Ranch/Malheur Wildlife Refuge in Oregon came down to the fact that the Bureau of Land Management and the Fish & Wildlife Service were working together to get farmers and ranchers to leave the area so that corrupt elements in the U.S. could get control of the land, then turn around and develop the property or sell water or mineral rights to politicians and wealthy businessmen.

Read *Hammond Case Facts* for the shocking story of what was happening to the Hammonds and other ranchers in southern Oregon for almost 20 years.[60] The Bureau of Land Management, a federal bureau, has been quietly taking away land from many sovereign states. Already, more than 63% of Nevada is owned by the federal government, a fact that flies in the face of states' rights, because states are supposed to retain ownership and control of their land.

---

60 *Hammond Case Facts - Ammon Bundy*. 3 Feb 2016. https://redoubtnews. com/2016/02/hammond-case-facts-ammon-bundy/.

The Bundys and the Hammonds were both painted by mainstream media as domestic terrorists who fostered events led by ignorant, aggressive men with ridiculous ideas and beliefs about a republic. Nothing could be further from the truth. The whole idea behind a successful republic is private ownership of land within independent states protected by an elected government. When a state loses ownership and control of its land, it ceases to exist. When a power-hungry group takes control of that land, you no longer have a republic, you have the makings of a dictatorship based on a feudal system of landowners and serfs, or in our case, on a system of corrupt corporations and renters. &

9

North Korea, Iran, and the Hawaii Missile

THE STANDOFF AT THE MALHEUR WILDLIFE REFUGE LED TO THE DISCOVERY of what was happening with American uranium, which then led to the discovery that uranium had been shipped in a very quietly circuitous manner from America to Canada to Europe to Iran and North Korea.[61]

When I discovered that Iran was building a secret nuclear facility in Syria with help from ISIS, I recalled a moment a few years earlier. In that moment, my sister-in-law was mentioning that she had gotten a sudden message from her son/my nephew who was in the military and had been sent to Turkey a number of times. We were always told that he was a helicopter repairman, and we knew he had been sent to Turkey more than once and returned without fanfare. Nothing was ever said about these trips, and we thought they were somewhat routine. However, on that most recent trip, my sister-in-law suddenly received an intense declaration of love from her son saying that if she didn't see him again, she should know he loved her. She commented that something must have happened that frightened him or shook him up and he wasn't certain that he was going to make it back home.

---

61 www.qmap.pub. Drop #1306, *Define Terms of Iran Nuclear Deal*. 30 April 2018.

This triggered one of those moments when a window opened in my consciousness and I could see that he did not appear to be in Turkey at all. He was somewhere to the south of Turkey and was involved in a clandestine operation that had little to do with repairing helicopters. It looked much more like he was ferrying supplies and equipment to somewhere in what I thought was Syria. "That's odd!" I thought to myself. "What would he be doing down there?" It appeared that he and his team had come under fire and had to fight their way back across the border to a safe zone. I dismissed the whole scene as very unlikely, but didn't forget it.

The discovery of Iran's secret project brought an instant, "Aha! *That* is the real reason for the invasion of Syria and the efforts to get rid of Bashar al Assad!" I already knew about the Cabal's "Seven Countries in Five Years" plan[62] and I was aware of the argument over the U.S.-backed pipeline vs. the Russia-backed pipeline. Russia wanted a pipeline to go from Iran through Iraq to Syria to Lebanon, and from there to Europe.

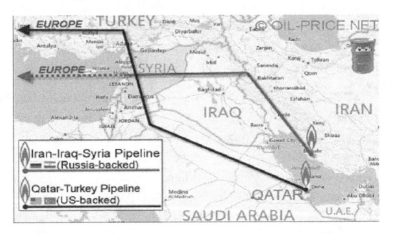

The U.S. wanted a pipeline to go from Qatar through Saudi Arabia and Jordan to Syria to Turkey and from there to Europe. The goal was to supply Europe with natural gas. But perhaps the whole pipeline argument was just a distraction to take attention away from the fact that Iran was building a nuclear plant in Syria.

---

62 FacelessWithEyesOpen. *General Wesley Clark: Wars Were Planned - Seven Countries in Five Years*. 11 Sept 2011. https://www.youtube.com/watch?v=9RC-1Mepk_Sw

Building a nuclear plant *outside* of Iran would get around those people *inside* Iran who were monitoring Iranian efforts to build nuclear plants that would supply electricity to the Iranian people. Obviously, if they were building a nuclear plant in Syria, they weren't planning to supply Iranians with electrical power. Were they planning to process uranium to weapons-grade level? And did they hope that by building in Syria, their secret plans and nuclear development program would escape detection?

"Why would Iran think it could just take over land in Syria?" I asked myself. Then it dawned on me. This was a perfect example of the Cabal's total disregard for nations and their borders. This was how they operated, and would continue to operate once they had full power—with deception and total disregard for what people wanted. Working things out peaceably was not their way. Pushing their will down everyone's throat was their way. Syria, like Iran and North Korea, was just another pawn.

In Q drop #1306, Q said that both Iran and North Korea were hostages of the Cabal and had secret nuclear missile programs being developed to start the next war. Not only was the Cabal supplying Iran and North Korea with uranium and helping them build nuclear plants that could enrich that uranium, it was giving them the blueprints needed to construct missiles, all with the intention of forcing them to use those nuclear arms to start wars or at least threaten to start wars.

Q post #29 noted: "Some things must remain classified to the very end. North Korea is not being run by Kim, he's an actor in the play. Who is the director? The truth would sound so outrageous most Americans would riot, revolt, reject, etc. The Pedo networks are being dismantled. The child abductions for satanic rituals (i.e. Haiti and other 3rd world countries) are paused (not terminated until players are in custody). We pray every single day for God's guidance and direction as we are truly up against pure evil."

Google CEO Eric Schmidt was helping North Korea to establish a highly classified communications system. This was to be used to send classified orders and perhaps handle missile control systems. However, Schmidt was tracked, photographed in the North Korean offices, and then confronted. He stepped down from his position immediately.

We do not know when Trump first contacted North Korea to notify them that there would be no further development of their nuclear program and to invite Kim Jong Un to meet and discuss getting out from under the control of the Deep State. However, on Nov. 2, 2017, Q post #41 reported:

> What a coincidence the mountain that housed North Korea's nuclear weapons and testing collapsed. Unbelievable timing. I wonder if critically important materials as well as scientists aka the bomb makers were inside when it happened. Shocking no global news agency suspects we had nothing to do with it. Enjoy the crumbs.

By the time Trump made his visit to meet with Kim Jong Un in North Korea in June 2018, most of their agreement had already been worked out. On his trip home, a missile was launched at Air Force One in an attempt to assassinate the President. The Cabal was planning to blame it on North Korea and use it as an excuse to start World War III. The missile was intercepted by F-16s with special equipment able to quickly target and take out missiles. Trump's plane was diverted and all was well.[63]

This was not the first time a missile was launched in this hidden fight. There were at least two others of note. One was an attempt to take down Air Force One in December 2017. That missile was also taken out. Another was in January of 2018 when residents of Hawaii were suddenly notified that there was an incoming missile and that the notice was not a practice drill, it was for real.

Later, Q revealed that the missile coming at Hawaii was deliberately launched and then just as deliberately taken down. However, during the time between the launch and the take down, something critically important was happening. Hawaii was the home of data servers containing highly classified information that was not duplicated on servers on the U.S. mainland. The Hawaiian servers were set up so that they were inaccessible to all except a very special few, then apparently they came under the control of the Cabal. The Q Team could not get access to this information

---

63 www.qmap.pub. Drop #2729, *Recall: Deep State Tried to Assassinate PO-TUS (AF1 Missile Strike) to Provoke War with NK,* 15 Feb 2019. Drop #1729, *F-16 Jets Intercepted Rogue Missile Launched at Air Force One,* 27 July 2018.

– *unless* there was a very real threat of an attack, at which point all of the data on the servers would be immediately and automatically transferred to the mainland! Thus, a missile was launched upsetting more than a few people in Hawaii, but then quickly taken down as soon as the data finished transferring. The Q Team had the information they needed.

☘

Before Trump even went to North Korea, he announced that he was going to be pulling out of the Iran deal and re-instituting sanctions, much to the dismay of France, Germany, and Britain.

"This resolution (the Iran Deal was officially known as the Joint Comprehensive Plan of Action) remains the binding international legal framework for the resolution of the dispute about the Iranian nuclear programme," British Prime Minister Theresa May, French President Emmanuel Macron and German Chancellor Angela Merkel said in their statement...Obama considered the Iran agreement a signature foreign policy accomplishment, calling it the best way to head off the near-term threat of a nuclear-armed Iran and a potential opening toward better relations with Tehran after more than three decades of enmity." [64]

The truth was that the Iran deal was never about Iran. It was a secret business deal to build the nuclear processing plant in Syria. Multi-million-dollar business deals had been made to supply the project. Macron, May, and Merkel were only upset about the disruption of those Cabal business deals, not the possibility of Iran becoming a country with nuclear power. Quite the opposite!

Obama and others in the U.S. political system also knew the truth about the Iran deal, yet they all lied through their teeth, glossing over the terms of the deal that "offered Tehran billions of dollars and sanctions relief in exchange for agreeing to curb its nuclear program. Officially, the

---

64 Gearan, Anne and DeYoung, Karen. *Trump pulls United States out of Iran nuclear deal, calling the pact 'an embarrassment'*. Washington Post. 8 May 2018. https://www.washingtonpost.com/politics/trump-will-announce-plans-to-pull-out-of-iran-nuclear-deal-despite-pleas-from-european-leaders/2018/05/08/4c148252-52ca-11e8-9c91-7dab596e8252_story.html?utm_term=.e2182d0a719d.

agreement was said to be aimed at ensuring that 'Iran's nuclear program will be exclusively peaceful.'" [65] In truth, the Iran deal was nothing more than a scam. It allowed Obama to send planeloads of money to Iran to continue building the secret nuclear plant in Syria.

The scam of sending billions of dollars to a country right *before* it was invaded, under the pretext of one deal or another, was common. When the invasion took place, banks would be the first to be raided and the money handily confiscated, usually to disappear in transit to hidden pockets and accounts elsewhere. Sending money right *after* an invasion, under the pretext of helping that country to rebuild, was also common. In this case, it would get lost in the confusion and end up with the same results. When we invaded Iraq, more than $12 billion was sent to help it rebuild. Somewhere along the way the money disappeared and only a small portion of it was ever recovered.[66] The attitude of the Cabal was that if it worked in Iraq, it would work in Iran.[67] They were planning to start a war with Iran and were sure they could get away with what they were doing until Trump came along. When Trump ended the deal and reinstated sanctions on Iran, his real goal was to spring Iran from the Cabal trap. Sanctions would make them much more open to discussions that would actually be in their favor.

Shortly after the decision to pull out of the Iran deal, Trump ordered the bombing of Syria and was met with a tremendous amount of criticism. The media made a circus out of this decision, criticizing him for attacking without a more comprehensive plan and for failing to consult with Congress.[68] Trump supporters suffered mightily at the thought that

---

65 Bruton, F. Brinley. *What is the Iran nuclear deal?* NBC News. 25 Apr 2018. https://www.nbcnews.com/storyline/smart-facts/what-iran-nuclear-deal-n868346

66 Risen, James. *Investigation Into Missing Iraqi Cash Ended in Lebanon Bunker*. New York Times, 12 Oct 2014. https://www.nytimes.com/2014/10/12/world/investigation-into-missing-iraqi-cash-ended-in-lebanon-bunker.html.

67 www.qmap.pub. Drop #2807, *Welcome to the Real World*. 19 Feb 2019.

68 Bendery, Jennifer. *Trump Bombs Syria Hours After 88 Lawmakers Urged Him to First Consult Congress*. HuffPost, 13 Apr 2018. https://www.huffingtonpost.com/entry/trump-military-strikes-syria-congressional-authorization_us_5ad117abe4b077c89ce89301.

they had been betrayed, it looked like peace was slipping further away and that Trump was acting like he was part of the New World Order. It was reported that the strikes were against Syrian research, storage, and military targets,[69] but what he really bombed was Iran's secret nuclear facility.[70]

By this time, it was becoming obvious that operations were proceeding as Q had said they would—first Saudi Arabia, then the U.S., then Asia, with Europe being cleaned up last. 80% of these operations would be hidden so that the majority of the public could go about their daily lives undisturbed and there would be a minimum of uproar.

I appreciated the efforts to fight the corruption without too much personal disruption, but the big risk was that hardly anyone knew what was really going on. This ignorance regarding what Trump was doing gave the Soros minions and mainstream media plenty of time to whip people into a frenzy again and again using tactics that divided us in every way possible—race, religion, sex, income, education, and whatever else they could think of.

During the time that Barack Obama was president and Hillary Clinton was Secretary of State, all manner of nefarious activities were going on in Washington DC. Barack Obama, son of a CIA operative, was a member of the Muslim religion and had been groomed to be president by Saudi Arabia. Saudi Arabia selected his cabinet members as well. Obama's handler was Valerie Jarrett, a Muslim, who worked as his top advisor and sniffer, making sure he got rid of anyone who might stand in their way.[71]

Huma Abedin, a long-time aide to Hillary Clinton, was also a Muslim, and so was James Brennan, head of the CIA.[72] People have argued

---

69 Ibid.

70 www.qmap.pub. Drop #1306, *Define Terms of Iran Nuclear Deal*. 30 April 2018.

71 www.qmap.pub. Drop #570, *The 16 Year Plan to Destroy America*. 21 January 2018.

72 www.qmap.pub. Drop #1887, *Obama Admin Protected ISIS, Al-Qaeda and Osama bin Laden*. 15 August 2018.

that we should ignore the fact that they are Muslim because it smacks of religious prejudice. However, accusations of religious prejudice should not be used to cloud the need for common sense and honest appraisals of what is happening. We cannot let fear of such accusations thwart political wisdom. To do so is a clear red flag that freedom has been lost and we have donned political straightjackets.

Obama, Jarrett, Abedin, Brennan, and others were working together to help bring down the U.S. The plan they were working from was to eventually implement Islam's Sharia law that demands all "Muslims are to subjugate the world under Islam…and should lie to advance or protect Islam."[73]

Obama was secretly bringing thousands of Muslims into the U.S. They came in late at night on UPS planes, disembarked, were herded quickly onto buses and taken immediately to various summer camps run by religious groups and non-governmental organizations. There they were assigned to cities and towns and given papers identifying them as U.S. citizens.[74] [75] Obama's goal was to create "seedling" communities of Muslims who would vote Democratic and rise up against U.S. citizens when called to do so.

At the same time that Muslim immigrants were secretly arriving by the thousands in the U.S., they were arriving by the millions in Europe, courtesy of George Soros who was responsible for handling populations, their brainwashing, and their movements. The influx of migrants into Europe caused a serious crisis in every country that allowed them in.

Although there was no honest mainstream media coverage in the U.S. regarding what was happening as a result of the migrant crisis in Europe, stories soon began to emerge in the alternative media about

---

73 *Sharia Law – List of Key Rules*. http://fourwinds10.com/siterun_data/ government/judicial_and_courts/sheria_law/news.php?q=1511023203 –

74 Still, Bill. *U.S. Taking 100k Muslim Refugees/Year*. Still Report #462. 28 Nov 2015. https://www.youtube.com/watch?v=KIf3tElDLfA

75 Still, Bill. *Obama is Still Planting Seedling Muslim Towns*. Still Report #866. 13 May 2016. https://www.youtube.com/watch?v=TD3Uh66YroM

rape, robbery, and all manner of ugly confrontations that were literally destroying European culture and economies. It is bad when an economy becomes unworkable, but when you lose your culture, you no longer have a population with the necessary cohesiveness to hold a nation together, which is exactly what Soros was trying to do. If he could collapse the culture, he could collapse the national boundaries.

Compared to the Muslim migrants in America, who seemed rather quiet, the migrant disruptions in Europe were working much better. To stir things up a little more in the U.S., Soros organized a migrant invasion by Central Americans into the U.S. He was now in a bit of a hurry because of the mounting pressures created by the Trump presidency to deal with the border. Soros, who was paying people in China $150/day to protest and $500/day to organize protests,[76] arranged to pay people to join the walkers headed to the U.S. border, and that is when the really serious arguments about the border wall began.[77]

America has a long history of being a nation of immigrants. As soon as the migrant situation started, the media began to present romantic views of immigration and sob stories that made people feel guilty if they didn't approve of open immigration. However, the open immigration they want only goes in one direction. They have been bringing people freely into the U.S. and making them full citizens, but you have to apply to leave the U.S. and pay money to get out of the citizenship. When people began leaving the U.S. in increasing numbers, the fee to renounce citizenship was jacked up 422% to $2,350, the highest in the world.[78]

When it comes to immigration, the media constantly draws attention away from discernment, common sense, and the need for the

76 *Jim Willie: Trump, Putin & Xi Secret reset Meetings to Beat the Globalists and Avoid WWIII.* Silver Doctors, 30 May 2019. https://www.youtube.com/watch?v=5-7b3E5Uv4c. (Start at 1:01:30 min.)

77 Still, Bill. *Soros Openly Giving Money to Migrants.* Still Report #2433, 4 Nov 2018. https://www.youtube.com/watch?v=xrN4OnKsDt4.

78 Wood, Robert. *U.S. Has World's Highest Fee to Renounce Citizenship.* Forbes, 23 Oct 2015. https://www.forbes.com/sites/robertwood/2015/10/23/u-s-has-worlds-highest-fee-to-renounce-citizenship/#326ce8847de3.

ordinary procedures that are in place to receive good people and turn away the bad. An immigrant is one thing, an intruder is something else, an invader is yet something else, and someone who is engaging in criminal deception with the intention of financial or personal gain is engaging in fraud.

Why would anyone want to ignore the fact that immigration is a *process* unless they were being dishonest? You have to apply, do paperwork, pay money, and get approval. In the same way that you can't just barge into someone's house and say, "I'm moving in. What time is dinner?" you can't just barge into a country and say, "I'm moving in. Where is the Welfare Office?" The whole message behind the Soros migrant invasions was and is, "We don't believe in nations and thus borders are irrelevant. We believe in a different kind of order and a new way of organizing ourselves into a one-world government." This, coupled with an absence of true information about the migrant-caused crises taking place in various European countries, has allowed the media to divide us in multiple ways.

Sadly, the actions of many in congress have only increased our own vulnerability. From their point of view, the border crisis has little to do with whether to build a wall or not, how to fund it or not, how to handle children at the border, how long to detain people trying to get in, whether we should return them to where they came from or let them in, whether to insist on proper procedures for obtaining citizenship or throw up our hands in overload, and whether or not to offer medical care, education, and welfare. Their goal was and is to keep us distracted, upset, and angry with one another—angry enough to not see the illegality of the things they are doing and have been doing for a very long time.

Their goal is to break up the U.S. and their attitude is that there's more than one way to get what they want. Working with the Cabal, their overarching goal is to collapse nations so they can install the globalist government of the New World Order. If they can't get rid of Trump and get back the power of the presidency through impeachment, they can still destroy our country by creating an ocean of confusion, misinformation, and division from which we do not recover.

℅

While Obama was president, he was working on the Muslim angle. Hillary Clinton was working on several angles—the Uranium One angle, the Clinton Foundation pay-for-play angle, and the "I'm gonna be the next president" angle.

While his cohorts were each coming at the takedown of the U.S. from their own angle of attack, John McCain was working on the ISIS angle. McCain was the man who organized and oversaw ISIS.[79]

I knew about McCain's Vietnam history long before the Q Team began dropping classified material on the 4chan board. I can still remember my shock when I happened to read an article on the *Veterans Today* blog in which Gordon Duff revealed that John McCain was not a war hero in Vietnam and that he was working with terrorists in the Middle East.[80] [81]

Those military men who knew that McCain was betraying the U.S. refused to use his name at all. He was referred to in the Q drops as "no-name." McCain was responsible for the organization, funding, recruitment, training, arming, mobilization, and direction of the mercenary fighters called ISIS. He promised the Islamic fighters some newly freed land on which they could eventually set up a caliphate. These were the men who were sent into Syria to take out Bashar al Assad. The media backed them up by reporting that the mercenaries were disgruntled Syrian rebels who disliked Assad and wanted to topple him. The truth is that they were McCain's recruited mercenaries, hired to get rid of Assad at all costs because the Cabal and their New World Order wanted control of that area.

Those military people on the Q Team who were loyal to the U.S. were particularly offended by McCain's treason. After Trump's election,

---

79 www.qmap.pub. Drop #732, *John McCain is a Traitor (Photo with ISIS Leaders)*. 11 February 2018.

80 Duff, Gordon. *NEO – How John McCain Crippled Obama's War on ISIS*. Veterans Today, 14 December 2015. https://www.veteranstoday.com/2015/12/14/neo-how-john-mccain-crippled-obamas-war-on-isis/

81 Alexis, Jonas E. *John McCain Received Money from Terrorist Regime Saudi Arabia*. Veterans Today, 2 April 2016. https://www.veteranstoday.com/2016/04/02/john-mccain-received-money-from-terrorist-regime-saudi-arabia/.

McCain realized the game was up. His brain tumor was announced publicly in July, 2017, and I assumed he concocted the story that he had been diagnosed with glioblastoma, an aggressive brain cancer, with the intention of faking his death. However, it appears that McCain was confronted by Trump's military team and given a choice: step down and go to your death quietly, or be exposed as a traitor. He chose to go quietly. The tumor story allowed him to linger a little while and get his affairs in order.

According to Q, McCain did not have brain cancer and never underwent surgery for it. The photos shown on CNN[82] and other media certainly made it look like he did, but given Hollywood's ability to simulate all manner of physical conditions, the scar could have been something he taped to his head. There is also the possibility that he was just cut open and then closed back up with nothing more than a surface cut in order to be as realistic as possible. It is difficult to say how he achieved the scar that supposedly resulted from the surgery.

After Q informed us that McCain's brain cancer was a charade, he gave us the exact date and time of McCain's death, and gave it to us a month before it happened.[83] The date and time were predictable because McCain was executed for treason by the military, who had set the date and time in advance. The truth about McCain was supposed to be buried with him in order to keep the country stable and to preserve his name and reputation as a hero in the public eye. This was undone when John Kasich, governor of Ohio, accidentally let the truth slip out with a press conference remark about "it only being 48 hours since John McCain was put to death."[84] Later, Q verified that McCain did not leave on his own terms.

---

82 Scutti, Susan. *Sen. John McCain has brain cancer, aggressive tumor surgically removed.* CNN, 20 July 2017. https://www.cnn.com/2017/07/19/health/gupta-mccain-glioblastoma/index.html.

83 www.qmap.pub. Drop #1649, *John McCain's Day is Coming*, 30 June 2018. Drop #1933, *John McCain Suicide Weekend (Proof)*. 26 August 2018.

84 *Watch: John Kasich Says "John McCain Was Put to Death."* SGT Report, 7 Sept 2018. https://www.sgtreport.com/2018/09/watch-john-kasich-says-john-mccain-was-put-to-death-video/.

We also learned through Q that the late June 2016 meeting on the tarmac between Bill Clinton and Loretta Lynch was originally planned as a secret meeting. However, the Q Team was already monitoring communications between members of the Deep State and alerted a couple of reporters that the meeting was to take place. Although Clinton and Lynch said the meeting was accidental and they only talked about grandchildren and golf, Q reported that the real discussion was Clinton's offer to give Lynch the seat on the Supreme Court vacated by the death of Antonin Scalia if Lynch would agree to go easy on Hillary in any investigation regarding her emails.[85]

Q also indicated that Antonin Scalia had been murdered because he was a conservative and the Democrats wanted to clear that space on the Supreme Court for a liberal judge. At first, I found it difficult to believe that Scalia was murdered except for several very unusual things that accompanied his death.

Scalia was reported to have had a heart attack even though he showed no signs of being uncomfortable or having difficulty at dinner. The heart attack is a common way of disposing of people and making it look blameless, as if the person died of natural causes when they really died because someone used a heart attack gun on them. The heart attack gun was a long-time secret weapon of the CIA and many people still do not know it exists.[86]

Another factor is that the autopsy was done by telephone! I laughed out loud when I heard that. I was sure it must be a mistake in reporting, but it turned out to be true. According to *The Atlantic*, "After Scalia was found, and law enforcement was on the scene, local justices of the peace were called to handle the inquest into his death. When no one was available, a county judge—who has the same inquest authorities as

85 www.qmap.pub. Drop #2860, *Tarmac Meeting Planned; Bill Offered Loretta a Supreme Court Seat if She Let Hillary Off the Hook*, 22 Feb 2019. Drop #2861, *Q Broke the News on Bill/Loretta Tarmac Deal; POTUS Later Confirmed by Tweet (Q Proof)*, 22 Feb 2019.

86 *The CIA's Secret Heart Attack Gun*. Military.com, 19 July 2013. https://www.military.com/video/guns/pistols/cias-secret-heart-attack-gun/2555371072001.

a justice of the peace—conducted the investigation over the phone."[87] So in reality, there was not really an inquest or an autopsy at all. It was just a phone conversation in which anyone could have said anything to make the judge believe that all was normal.

Anyone planning to eliminate Scalia would have done their homework carefully because of his position on the Supreme Court. Texas would have been a very good place to carry out the murder, especially such a remote area of Texas without a county medical examiner. Scalia was invited to join the hunt at the luxury resort named Cibolo Creek Ranch, which had something of a reputation for secret parties a la Bohemian Grove and Rent Boy Ranch.

When placed against a backdrop of the 65 or more people on the Clinton *body bag list*, and Hillary's campaign for a presidency that she never expected to lose, it was difficult to dismiss the idea that Scalia was murdered because Hillary had decided to put someone in place who had already proved her willingness to go along with the Cabal program, a liberal who would promise to overlook the crimes of Hillary Clinton, a liberal like Loretta Lynch. ✺

---

87 Kelly, Nora. *Why Wasn't Antonin Scalia Given an Autopsy?* The Atlantic, 17 Feb 2016. https://www.theatlantic.com/politics/archive/2016/02/antonin-scalia-autopsy/463251/.

10 ✀

It's Not a Game

WHILE THE CABAL DID HAVE A HEADSTART AND A LOT OF POWER, THEY never thought Hillary would lose the election so they never put together a complete and comprehensive plan of action in case she lost. When they saw the number of people showing up at rallies for Hillary and compared that to the number of people showing up for Donald Trump rallies, they weren't worried because they were planning to rig the voting machines. Little did they know that military intelligence was well aware of the rigging that had been going on in previous elections and was planning to go around behind Cabal backs and reset those same machines in order to get an honest election.

Although those in the Hillary camp didn't think she would lose, they did go so far as to order and pay for a fake dossier on Trump—just in case. However, their assumption that they could use the dossier to threaten Trump with impeachment and get rid of him the same way they got rid of Nixon was based on an outdated understanding of the American people.

The Cabal view of Americans was that they were slow, ignorant, lazy, and would believe whatever they were told. Unfortunately for the Cabal, 35 years of internet experience had changed the American mindset far more than they realized. The Cabal ought to have taken heed of Admiral

Yamamoto's comment upon bombing Pearl Harbor, "I fear all we have done is to awaken a sleeping giant and fill him with a terrible resolve."

Yes, the corporate-banking Cabal was using the internet to spy on us, track our purchases and activities, and manipulate our desires and perceptions. However, we were using the internet to see into the hidden workings of the corporate-banking Cabal and their attempt to take over our government. We were communicating with one another about what we were seeing and suspecting on a far wider basis than before. We were using the internet to read, watch, and listen to the arguments, theories, reports, and stories that had been officially reported, then comparing those reports to the reports of real folks who had been present at these events, people who saw and heard what really went on and was actually said.

We were recognizing big patterns of deceit that unfolded over a longer period of time than we had formerly observed. We were sharing perceptions, experience, observations, thoughts, worries, hopes, dreams, potentials, and plans in ways that greatly sharpened our awareness of how technology could be used—and used against us.

The internet captured millions of photo-and-audio moments in which politicians on the campaign trail made specific promises and then did the exact opposite once they were in office. In the old days, people would attend a live speech or watch a televised speech, and once it was over, it was over. It could not be easily replayed. Whatever differences there were between the promises made and the actual behavior became fuzzy and uncertain because memory was often fuzzy and uncertain. The library was the only place to go to dig up old newspapers that might have reported the speech correctly, and no one had time to chase such information because we were too busy working, too stressed about money, and too naive to think that such magnificent politicians would mislead us or lie.

But! Every change in this world is a two-edged sword. The internet, symbol of the global mind, of the telepathy going on continuously among billions of brains, had fundamentally changed our consciousness in ways that the Cabal failed to recognize. We were waking up, and as Q pointed out many times, "Their biggest fear is that you will awaken."

The internet matured us a little. At the very least, its presence taught us that we could communicate anywhere in space and time. It took us past our collective stage as a nation of 3-year-olds passively watching the governmental cartoon happening in print and on-screen, to interacting in vibrant, creative ways and posting our own views and stories to that screen, all of which increased our power to share, develop our ideas, and have a say in everything going on.

In the Cabal mind, power was to be used to control others, usually in negative ways. It was used to force others to do as the authorities demanded. Perhaps they believed that the only reason for having power was so that they could use it to greedily manipulate and deceive.

Those of us outside the Cabal were NOT using power in negative ways; we were simply sharing and communicating, which changes consciousness in many and subtle ways. Thus, the Cabal never saw the power of the common man coming at him until it blew up in their faces with the election of Donald Trump.

The Cabal used everything they had via the Internet and media in their efforts to beat Trump. When Trump won and Hillary did not give a concession speech wishing the new administration good luck, I was surprised. The reason she never conceded was because she was planning to unseat Trump using the Fusion GPS dossier and the Russian collusion story. In her mind, there was no reason to concede. The election was just a temporary interruption in her plan. Soon Trump would be gone and she would step into her imagined role as the rightful leader of the American people.

Looking back, it is clear that as the bankers and corporations that made up the Cabal worked the long coup and got closer and closer to success, they became over-confident and sloppy. They miscalculated us, and they miscalculated the effects of too many false flags. It didn't take long to figure out their pattern of using false flags to distract people from news that was extremely relevant to the population of a healthy republic. It is difficult to say what made them think the blatant use of symbolism that trumpeted their worship of Satan would be missed or overlooked. It was even more preposterous for them to think we would overlook their assumed license to engage in sordid activities such as pedophilia and child sex trafficking, or outcomes such as that suffered by little Jonbenet Ramsey. It took a long time to see their patterns of manipulation, longer to become certain that something ugly was afoot, longer yet to be able to predict what was going to happen next with any kind of confidence, and even longer to find others who were seeing the same patterns and their outcomes...but we did it!

ℏ

In the beginning, the autists and many of those reporting what was going on behind the scenes in the Trump camp were slow to grasp the finer implications of the Q messages. They wanted to see some action and insisted that Hillary should be dangling from the end of a rope *right now*! But judges and lawyers who have been paid to make certain decisions do not care about justice and fairness under the law. The autists failed to realize that her case would be quickly dismissed if corrupt judges and lawyers were not removed from the court system first. This meant having to wait for elections to happen and appointments to be approved.

If it had been up to some autists and many in the public, the whole fight would have been lost from the start. We were not very good poker players and would have played our entire hand in the first month and then been wiped out, outsmarted at every turn. We didn't see the need to set things up properly. We lacked any appreciation of strategic moves and were thoroughly upset when Q said such-and-such was going to happen," and then it didn't—because it was deliberate disinformation meant to confuse the Cabal.

Early in the drops, we were warned that we would have to cope with disinformation. In spite of the warning, it took a while for the autists and analysts to catch on. Many of them would become uncertain that anything real was going to come of their efforts to decode the cryptic messages dropped by Q.

The autists also seemed unaware that members of the Cabal might be closely watching the Q messages. They failed to assess the effect of false information on the Cabal psyche and did not understand that the Q team did not want to telegraph their moves to enemies who were quietly watching those drops in order to glean information about the President's next moves. When something didn't happen the way Q said it would, there was uproar on the boards.[88]

As I watched all of us, from the autists, to those intrepid men and women reporting and analyzing the results put out by the autists, it was clear that the American public had been woefully programmed for decades by their experience with movies. It took many people forever to recognize that the fight was not going to be a cops-and-robbers action drama that would end in an hour and a half. Even more unrealistically, many people expected events to come to a sparkling conclusion in which the bad guys were rounded up and marched off to jail while triumphant music played in the background and the good guys smiled and slapped one another on the back, because, of course, the good guys always won.

When this did not happen, many became impatient. A year after the first Q posts came out, autists complained that they didn't expect that the task of having to track and/or figure out Q's messages was going to go on this long. They joked about having given up their life in order to stick with the continuous need for research and decoding messages.Many complained that family and friends had abandoned them for supporting Trump. They were not prepared for the long haul. They failed to see that it was all being conducted using the rule of law and the constitution — because restoring the rule of law was the point of the entire effort.

Another complaint made by some inside the Q movement, as well as outside, was that "nothing has happened." They said this because they wanted to see arrests right now! They continued to do a spectacular job, but I noted with dismay how tired and discouraged they became. Their YouTube videos were often de-monetized and taken down by the Google gestapo for frivolous reasons. The number of views they received would mysteriously be cut to a handful. Those who followed them would discover that notices of a new posting were never received or would end up in the subscribers' junk mail. The audio on some videos was tampered with. Certain words used in the video triggered the elimination of the

---

88 4Chan.net and 8Chan.net

video from a search, and some channels were outright banned or hidden from the public altogether.

There were periods of utter silence from the Q team, and during these times, the shills were especially active. A perfect example of shilling was from @XKeyscore who said: "I have not seen one #TicToc prediction go down. 70,000+ sealed indictments, arrests and #GITMO? #QAnon is a #PSYOP & the '10 Days of Darkness' line comes from Blade Runner 2049. I wish #Q had substance but so far: ZILCH. Q is a conservative-placating mechanism."

Between the shills and the mainstream media, I swung between hope and doubt, never sure that things were going to be resolved in favor of truth, honesty, and justice. Each time Q was silent for a period of time, I went back to mainstream media to see what they were saying. And each time I did so, my anger with the them mounted quickly to a fury.

"How dare you lie and twist and spin!!" I raged inwardly at them. "You should be ashamed! You are supposed to be reporting unbiased news so we can make wise choices in managing our government. But no! You took the privileges we offered and ran off with them while spewing crap to the people. You may get your way, dammit, the U.S. may collapse, but by god, so will you. Your betrayal will not be forgiven. Your time is over. And what will you have to show for it? Nothing!"

In addition to the cool lies of mainstream media, I was often upset by the anxious impetuousness of many Trump supporters reading the Q drops. After a while, it was clear that the biggest problem with the Q information was not really with Q or the information, it was with people's perception. Very few had the clarity or the ability to track the moves being made and then ask, "If that is what we see on the surface, what happened behind the scenes to drive that action?"

&

No one ever knows how long a situation will go on, and thus a common problem is failure to conserve energy as much as possible. The tension was exhausting at every level, physically, mentally, and emotionally. When spirits flagged, Q thanked the autists and everyone else, encouraging all, telling both autists and patriots they were doing a great job. Somehow, everyone kept going with a deep spirit of adventure and insight. When a fight saps your spirit, you have lost.

When my spirit sagged, I asked myself the hard questions a hundred times. "Are we being fooled into taking no action? Are we being led to believe somebody is standing up and saying something? Are we being saved from the grip of the Cabal? Is the country going to survive? Or is the whole Q thing an elaborate virtual reality game and we are being played like suckers? Is there any way to get evidence that what they *say* is happening is really happening?"

I decided to go back to the beginning, re-read all of the Q drops, and look at whatever evidence we had so far. If it became obvious that the whole thing was a LARP,[89] then so be it. I was willing to face the hard truth if that's what it came down to, however...

The arrests of more than two dozen of the most powerful people in Saudi Arabia and the declaration of marshal law in that country was not a game.

The plane crash in the yard of the Rothschilds was not a game.

The unexplained murders that the mainstream media reported as suicides of more than a dozen people found hanging from doorknobs, including Anthony Bourdain and Kate Spade, was not a game.

The argument over building a wall to stop the attempted invasion of the U.S. by thousands upon thousands of illegal immigrants was not a game.

The treasonous behavior by the Democrats and some RINOS was not a game.

The Las Vegas massacre was not a game.

The photos I had seen of a dead black child with a couple of proud hunters standing over the body just like deer hunters pose over their dead deer was not a game.

---

89 LARP = Live Action Role Play.

The murder of Antonin Scalia was not a game.

The execution of John McCain on the exact day and time predicted by Q was not a game.

The minister who addressed Hillary Clinton as Madame President at John McCain's funeral was not a game.

The death of George H.W. Bush as signaled by James Comey two weeks before it was publicly announced, and the funeral being set for the exact date that had been set for exposure of the corruption in the Clinton Foundation was not a game. Nor was the change in attitude and the shocked demeanor that occurred among those present at the funeral when they opened mysterious envelopes hidden within their program folders.

The take-down of multiple communication satellites used by the cabal was not a game.

The incoming missile headed for Hawaii in order to transfer data to the mainland and the Trump team was not a game.

The fact that the Clinton Foundation donations dropped to nothing the minute Hillary lost the election was not a game.

The fact that the Clinton Foundation's non-profit status only allowed them to take in money for the Clinton Library. The fact that they took in millions for Haiti earthquake relief and only sent Haiti enough money to build five little pre-fab houses was not a game.

Bill Clinton's meeting with Loretta Lynch on the tarmac in Arizona and his offer to give her Scalia's seat on the Supreme Court if she would make sure that the investigation into Hillary's emails went nowhere was not a game.

The fact that Seth Rich downloaded DNC information onto a thumb drive and gave it to WikiLeaks and then was murdered by MS13 members—who were themselves then murdered so they couldn't talk—was not a game.

The fact that Bruce Ohr and Andrew McCabe had been stone-walling all efforts to get to the bottom of the FBI's spying on candidate and then President Trump was not a game.

The fact that Bruce Ohr's wife, Nellie, spoke Russian and worked for Fusion GPS involving the Russian collusion story was not a game.

The fact that Tony Podesta let go of all his employees and closed down his entire lobbying company then got on a plane in an attempt to leave the country only to have the plane be forced to turn around or be shot down was not a game.

The fact that the Russian executive who knew the details of the Uranium One deal was killed, along with 150 innocent people who were on the plane with him, was not a game.

The fact that Hollywood stars were speaking up about the rotten core of pedophilia and sex trafficking in Hollywood was not a game.

The arrest of Clare Bronfman, Keith Raniere, and Allison Mack for their involvement in the NXIVM (pronounced nex-ium) sex slave cult was not a game.

The fact that Hillary Clinton had paid someone tens of thousands of dollars to compile a dossier containing a pack of lies about Donald Trump and Russia was not a game.

The fact that the FBI had used those lies to obtain a FISA court warrant to spy on Donald Trump both before and after his election was not a game.

The fact that there were now over 80,000 sealed indictments when the norm was a couple thousand per year was not a game.

The sudden retirement of Paul Ryan, Cory Booker, John Conyers, and Eric Schmidt, who had suddenly aborted very successful or promising careers, was not a game.

The fact that thousands of corrupt politicians, businessmen, scientists, and academics had stepped down from their positions after being confronted with evidence of their corruption was not a game.

The fact that North Korea had agreed to de-nuclearize was not a game.

The collapse of an entire mountain housing scientists working on North Korea's nuclear program, killing them all, was not a game.

The attempt of thousands of illegal immigrants to get into the U.S. without going through the proper processes was not a game.

The whistleblowers who kept coming forward to try to tell us that something was wrong in the departments and agencies they worked in were not playing a game.

The fact that thousands of Muslims had been brought into the country and Muslim communities were suddenly springing up or expanding rapidly was not a game.

The fact that the Vatican was embroiled in numerous scandals involving pedophilia, money laundering, and other criminal activities was not a game.

The fact that Facebook was surveilling the population continuously was not a game.

The fact that Julian Assange was captive in the Ecuadorian embassy in England for seven years was not a game.

The fact that children were being kidnapped around the world and sold for nefarious purposes was not a game.

The list of over 65 people who got in the way of Hillary and Bill Clinton and ended up dead was not a game.

The presence of several ISIS training camps in the U.S. was not a game.

The intent of the Cabal to collapse national borders and take over the entire world was not a game.

There were other factors that were extremely serious, but as is my habit, I kept an open mind. It didn't look like we were being played for suckers, but the situation was far from over. Unfortunately, as I was soon to discover, there was much more to be concerned about than Trump, Q, the government, or the possibility we were being played for suckers. ✄

11 ❧

The Nova Cycle

QUESTIONS ABOUT WHAT WAS GOING ON IN OUR COUNTRY CONTINUED TO come up and I continued to wrestle with doubt and hope. One day would be up and the next day down. When the questions came up, I tried to brush them aside. As autumn headed into winter, I kept having the feeling that something big, something unalterable was coming.

Just after Thanksgiving, we received word that the father of my children had been diagnosed with lung cancer. He was a smoker for 50 years and there was so much COPD damage to his lungs that they could not take out the lung with the cancer because the other lung was not healthy enough to support the body on its own. Worse, he had an infection in the cancerous lung that turned out to be MRSA. The infection was at the bottom of the lung, below the cancer, and antibiotics were not reaching it. We already knew he had a large abdominal aneurysm that kept him on the precipice of life, but this new information threw the entire family into chaos.

Melissa, my second-oldest daughter, flew to Las Vegas immediately in hopes of being able to help, but he died on Christmas Eve. We all cried, but for Melissa it was a pain so great that I was afraid for her. She sobbed uncontrollably for weeks and lashed out at everyone. We all knew that she was her father's favorite and she loved him unconditionally. Nothing we said helped. For us, her grief was almost more excruciating than the loss of the man who had been so much a part of our lives. We all felt helpless in the face of such pain.

In an effort to get some relief from the pain of loss and get a better grip on my life, I got on the treadmill one evening and took my iPad with me. I thought I would get away from family drama, political news, and Q drops to watch something new and different, maybe some of my favorite science or math channels.

I turned on YouTube, and like a creature of habit, browsed through the science channels I loved. I clicked on one that I had visited before. It was one whose information I kept trying to get my mind around— MaverickStar Reloaded.

In the video, a young man from England was reporting on the position of the north pole. It had been moving slowly for some time, maybe a few kilometers per year. Then it began to move more quickly in a fairly straight line, leaving northern Canada, crossing the Arctic Ocean, and traveling into Siberia at the galloping rate of 50 kilometers per year!

In most of his videos, the young Englishman would point to where the pole was currently positioned and say, "It is moving toward the 40-degree latitude mark, and we all know what that means!" Sometimes he would say it a little differently, "It's almost to the 40-degree point, and we know what will happen when that occurs!"

I had been watching his videos for more than a year and for most of that time, this comment frustrated me because I *didn't* know what would happen at the 40-degree mark, and I never had the time to go look it up. I assumed he was hinting at something bad, but I also assumed that he was like everyone else on YouTube—dramatizing stories in order to get people to visit his channel. Still, he seemed more down to earth, more serious than others.

He was also willing to constantly review, correct, and update his observations, something that I appreciated after my years of working with Dr. Wm. Levengood in his lab. Science is a dynamic affair and all attempts to cram a theory into a box will eventually fail.

I was highly aware of the tendency of amateurs to jump to conclusions about scientific information and what it meant. Levengood used to say, "Don't make premature cognitive commitments. If you don't know yet, then you don't know yet. Just keep researching and studying. If you are patient, thorough, and allow the data to stand and speak for itself, eventually the answers will fall right into your lap."

On this particular night, when it was obvious that the young Englishman was not going to explain what would happen when the North Pole reached the 40-degree latitude mark, I looked for something else that might be interesting.

When I came across a video with a title that went something like, *The Cause of Ice Ages*, I clicked on it because I was interested in the ongoing argument about climate change. It turned out to be part of a lecture series by Douglas Vogt who was presenting information he had put together about the real cause of ice ages.

❧

Originally, Doug Vogt was not a scientist. He was an accountant. Early in his life he owned a small publishing company that specialized in publishing scientific works. He began reading many of the scientific papers, books, and materials he was publishing and became interested in astronomy and the stars. He started making a database of the distance from Earth to various stars. As time went on, he noticed that there were no stars in the region that was 11,742 light years (LY) away. There were none at 23,810 light years away, or at a distance of 35,878 light years. There were none at 47,945 light years, none at 59,360 light years, and none at the 71,428 light year point. This intrigued him.

Most of these blank spots were almost exactly 12,068 years apart. Only the one at 59,360 light years was different, but not by much. It was only 11,415 light years from the previous one, a difference that was 653 years earlier than the rest. Vogt started trying to figure out why the empty bands of stars existed and why they were 12,068 years apart. It wasn't long before he realized that it only *appeared* there were no stars at those distances. The stars were there, but they couldn't be seen because they were obscured behind dust clouds that blocked the stars from view. The question then became, What was creating massive dust clouds every 12,068 years?

What he eventually discovered was that every 12,068 years, our sun—our star—undergoes a nova. At the time that Vogt reached his conclusion about the sun's nova process, scientists believed that a star going through a nova was always destroyed. This destruction might be true for a supernova, however, Vogt recognized that stars had to be going through a weaker version of a nova that did not destroy them. He called it a micro-nova and concluded that in this process, a star was merely blowing off the dust, debris, and rocky matter that it had accumulated over the previous 12,068 years. Fascinated by the regularity of the process, he set out to look for physical evidence of this recurring event. Not only did he find an abundance of evidence, he ended up answering a number of questions from other fields of science that had gone unanswered for decades, even a centuries.

The micro-nova, a gigantic poof that was sort of like a solar sneeze, created a compression wave that took about 8 minutes to reach the earth. The energy of this sneeze was charged with high-powered radiation. This radiation included cosmic rays, gamma rays, and serious ultraviolet frequencies that would hit the earth, the moon, and every other planet in the solar system. For those of us on Earth, such a hit would immediately take out the electric grid leaving all of us in the dark.

In Vogt's lecture series,[91] he then reminds us of Boyle's Law, something we learned in 9th grade science. When you compress a gas, its temperature goes *up*, and when you expand a gas, its temperature goes *down*.

The pressure of this wave hitting the earth greatly compressed the atmosphere (a combination of gases) on the side of the planet facing the sun, causing temperatures to go up dramatically, as high as 1,500-2,000 degrees Fahrenheit. Between the sudden temperature increase and the cosmic radiation, everything on the sun-facing side of the Earth was

91 Vogt, Douglas. *Causes of the Ice Age and Nova, the Greatest Secret of the United States, Series 4, Part 1, What causes the Ice Age.* 9 Nov 2018. https://www.youtube.com/watch?v=bMr-5HHnAmU&t=11s.

burned to a crisp and massive amounts of ocean water were evaporated from the surface of the ocean, lowering ocean levels between 400 ft and 1,200 ft.

This initial solar flash and wave of radiation was followed about 17 hours later by a massive cloud of dust, stony materials, and other debris moving through the solar system. The cloud of debris traveled at enormous speeds of 1,550 miles/second and when it hit the Earth, it pulverized whoever and whatever happened to be on the side facing the sun at that moment.

When the cloud of pulverizing dust hit, it would blow away the atmosphere on the sun-facing side of the planet and Boyle's Law would come into play again, this time because the atmosphere on the far side of the planet *not* facing the sun quickly *expanded* to fill in evenly around the entire planet. This rapid expansion caused winds of tremendous speeds that scoured the surface of the earth and caused the temperatures to drop precipitously into the range of -200 degrees Fahrenheit, flash freezing everything on the spot.

Thus, there would be fires burning on one side of the planet, and flash-freezing on the other. In addition to the flash freezing, there would be sudden reductions of breathable oxygen, partly because the atmosphere had been blown away, partly because the out-of-control fires used a great deal of oxygen, and partly because the expansion of the atmosphere around the globe caused a temporary thinning of breathable air.

When the initial solar flash first hit the earth, it would slow or even stop the rotation of the earth for a few hours. At the equator, the Earth and her oceans rotate about 1000 mph and any slowing or stopping of that rotation would cause the water to come up out of its basin and roll across the continents in a fast-moving wave.

Even though there was a theory that just before the sun's nova, the Earth's rotation would slow down because the magnetic field around the planet dropped to a very low level...and even though the speed of rotation drops off as you move north or south away from the equator...and even though tons of water from the ocean may have been evaporated by the heat of the initial solar flash, there would still be more than enough water to destroy coastlines and civilizations on every continent.

The drop in the magnetic field around the Earth and the slowing of the rotation could also cause the north and south poles to reverse positions. The magnetic field is what causes the Earth to rotate. When magnetic north is up at the top of our planet, as it is currently, we rotate to the left or in a counterclockwise direction, from west to east. If magnetic north reversed and went to the bottom of the Earth, the planet would begin rotating in the opposite direction, from east to the west. The sun would then come up in the west.

Any drop in the magnetic field would create other difficulties. The weight of the ice at the north and south poles is held in place by the rotation of the Earth. If the planet stopped rotating, or even slowed down, the ice packs at the poles would tend to tip the planet over until the ice ends up at the equator or finds a new balance point. This would create an entirely new north and south pole and a new axis of rotation, which would, in turn, create massive increases in volcanic activity and earthquakes. Between the dust from the sun's nova and the ash from volcanoes, the sun would be greatly obscured for years, even decades.

Changes in the rate of rotation, the location of the poles, or the location of the axis around which the planet rotated would also cause intense pressures on the planet that could destabilize the crust and cause continents to break up or crash into one another.

There were other possibilities that could occur during a nova event. The blast wave could push our planet a little further from the sun, changing our orbit and the length of our year.

The evaporation of 400–1,200 ft. of water from the surface of the ocean would create the next problem in the form of rain and snow. For the first week after the nova, a hot rain would fall. As the temperature dropped, the rain would turn to snow in the colder areas, which would be greatly expanded because of the dust obscuring the sun. The rain would flood everything that wasn't flooded by the rampaging oceans, and the snow would bury everything in whatever areas happened to end up more than 20 degrees latitude north or south of the equator. Snow and ice have even been recorded as far south as Mexico.

According to Vogt, the rain would come down for weeks, and the amount of snow that would fall would likely be in the range of 19,000 ft. deep. This snow would eventually compact into ice, and we would have the start of a new ice age. Rain and snow would continue until the huge amounts of water that evaporated into the atmosphere were used up.

In one of his lectures, Vogt mentioned that we would begin to notice several things about the sun shortly before the nova event. One was that it would change color from yellow to a very whitish color. Another was that it would begin to swell and the moon would no longer cover the entire surface of the sun during a solar eclipse. Eventually the sun would swell so much that an eclipse of the sun by the moon would resemble an old-fashioned, white sidewall tire. We would no longer be able to see only the corona of the sun in a full eclipse.

Said Vogt, "We have a little climate warming right now because the sun is beginning to swell. The warming has nothing to do with people or what they're driving or burning, and it has nothing to do with CO_2 levels. If nobody was on the planet, we would still see the same thing."[92]

Geologists had been asking for many years why there was a pronounced layer of black soot on everything that occurred about 12,000 years ago and showed up in the ice cores. Others wondered why the continents seemed to have moved and how that might have happened. Paleontologists had been asking why thousands of plants, animals, and trees had been shredded then buried and frozen in mud in the arctic regions. Astronomers had wondered why the moon was pockmarked with tiny dust craters, as if someone had thrown a handful of large pebbles at it with considerable force. They wondered what had happened to the water on Mars when it was obvious there had once been lots of water on that tiny, red planet. Climatologists had long advanced many theories about how and why the ice ages started and how they ended, but no one really knew.

---

92 Vogt, Douglas. *Causes of the Ice Age, Series 4, Part 3 - What Happens to the Oceans.*" 14 Dec 2018. https://www.youtube.com/watch?v=m-g4Xt-VVzA&t=3085s .

Vogt pointed out that when scientists studied ice core samples, they noticed a big increase in carbon dioxide associated with the start of an ice age. This increase of carbon dioxide was likely due to the massive fires that resulted from the sun's nova, since carbon dioxide is a by-product of burning carbon-based materials.

Vogt found there were places on Earth where the fierce initial blast of cosmic rays and gamma rays had melted and glazed the surface of the soil and turned it into glass. There were also glass spherules and nano-diamonds scattered across the eastern half of North America. These materials could only have been formed by intense heat while spinning at a high rate of speed on the long journey from the sun to the Earth. The glass spherules had what are known as fission tracks in them—tiny, pinpoint-sized tubules created by radiation in the form of fast-moving particles known as cosmic rays. These particles hit and pierced the spherules, leaving their tracks in the form of tubules.[93]

The same glass materials with fission tracks were found on the moon showing that it had been in the path of the sun's blast as well. Vogt contends that the U.S. government only sent men to the moon to look for evidence of the sun's nova cycle. As soon as they analyzed the rocks and soil samples brought back from the moon, they knew that they were looking at evidence of a blast of debris from the sun. They had what they wanted and did not plan any further trips, eventually canceling the entire NASA program.

There was still other evidence. Along the edges of every continent on the planet, erosion had cut deep, long canyons into the edges of those continents. Scientists had long wondered how these erosions occurred when the land was already under water. To Vogt, it was clear that these eroded canyons were created by ocean water that had left its basin, inundated the land, then rushed back over the edge of continents creating huge erosions as it returned to the ocean basins, signaling that the catastrophe was beginning to end.

---

93 Vogt, Douglas. *Causes of the Ice Ages, Series 4, Part 2, Scientific Proof the Sun Novas*. 3 Dec 2018. https://www.youtube.com/watch?v=PS_yq19Af-s&t=15s.

Papers had been written over the years by archaeologists who said there was evidence of very advanced cultures that existed thousands of years before the Sumerians and Egyptians.What happened to them? Paleontologists studying the shredded bodies of animals, fish, and trees frozen in the mud of the Alaskan tundra kept asking, "What could have caused such violence?" There were many woolly mammoths, all frozen in deep, homogenous layers of ice and mud in Northern Canada and Siberia. Some of these mammoths died with flowering plants in their stomachs, indicating they had been peacefully grazing in a temperate climate when they were suddenly suffocated in 90 feet of mud and flash frozen for thousands of years. Always the question had been asked, "What happened that killed such big animals and so quickly froze them, packing all in deep layers of *homogenous* mud? The evidence of a massive cataclysm on the planet was everywhere. Until Doug Vogt, no one had put it all together.

Let's correct that statement. There was one other person who had put it together. His name was Chan Thomas, and somewhere in the 1950s or early 60s, he wrote a 250-page book titled *The Adam and Eve Story*. He, too, put the pieces together. However, the CIA confiscated his book, classified it as top secret, and released a highly sanitized version of it a few years later. The book had the same title, and Thomas was given credit as the author, but the new version was only 57 pages long.

Doug Vogt had most of his theory pieces assembled by 1977, but he didn't publish it until 2007 in a book titled *God's Day of Judgment*. In it, he described the nova event and said it was a regular part of what he called the Clock Cycle—the regular effort of the solar systems in the universe to renew, regenerate, and re-synchronize themselves.

The CIA telephoned Vogt after he came out with his book and asked, "How did you figure it out?" They wanted to meet with him. He kindly refused the invitation. If he had told them how he figured it out and what his sources were, it is likely those sources would have disappeared in an effort to make sure no one else would be able to figure out what some are now calling *the catastrophe cycle*.

Doug Vogt is Jewish and studied the Hebrew alphabet for many years before he discovered that the letters of the Hebrew alphabet were not really letters at all. Their shapes represented the shape of plasma energy as it moved through various positions around the torus of magnetic energy surrounding the Earth. He also studied the Bible in depth and uncovered the fact that much of the information about the Clock Cycle was encoded in the first five books of the Bible. The Sumerians and other ancient people knew about this recurring catastrophe and called it "God's Day of Judgment." They considered the sun to be the Lord of the solar system, and called the catastrophe "The Day of the Lord."

Douglas Vogt presented this information in a clear and even understated manner, but the information was blockbuster in nature. By the time I got off the treadmill, I was in a state of shock. &

12 &

Beautiful and Terrifying

OVER THE NEXT FEW WEEKS, I FOUND THE REST OF DOUG VOGT'S LECTURES and watched almost all of them. I ordered and read three of his books, looking for some flaw in his theory, but the more I read, the more I recognized that he was right. He was coming at all of the science from a new and unbiased direction, and he had not been indoctrinated by the educational system's standard versions of astronomy, physics, geology, archeology, or paleontology. Other scientists had come up with pieces, but Vogt put them all together. At the time he came up with his theory, he was not an academic who needed to publish in order to get tenure, nor was he a scientist who needed to watch what he said in order to get funding. He was piecing together information from a half-dozen disciplines without thought of having to protect territory or status.

Between the time Vogt put together his information and the time he published it, he continued to survey the published papers in science and at first wondered why other scientists were not figuring it out. Later he realized that anyone putting out anything that came close to uncovering the sun's nova cycle was just not getting published. A few scientists hinted at the nova cycle, but no one came right out and said it.

In addition to his theory about the sun's nova process, Vogt developed a Theory of Multidimensional Reality based on information as the basic building block of our cosmos. I was surprised to see how closely his theory matched my own Theory of Consciousness. He postulated eight dimensions, whereas I had outlined four dimensions: Mind/Space, Consciousness/Energy, Intelligence/Particle, and Intent/Pattern. However, if I combined his eight dimensions into four, then his descriptions of his eight aligned to a surprising degree with the descriptions of my four. This made it hard to discount what he was saying.

I also had a decent understanding of plasma physics thanks to the many years spent working with Dr. Wm. Levengood. The places where I thought Vogt was reaching for an explanation were places that were easily explained by plasma, and his efforts to integrate information about the soul were easily explained by consciousness. The individual soul was simply a small region of frequencies and fields in Mind/Space that had evolved to become a cohesive form.

Vogt's information was both beautiful and terrifying. It was beautiful because it matched real observations and answered so many long-standing questions about anomalous events on our planet. It was terrifying because of what it said was coming at us.

A search using the terms *solar flash event* turned up a surprisingly broad selection of websites talking about a solar flash. I went back and listened to a couple of lectures by Paul LaViolette, in hopes of hearing what he had to say with new ears. However, after listening to Vogt's elegant explanation, LaViolette's theory of an explosion in the center of the galaxy that created a superwave of dust moving through the galaxy sounded like an overdone piece of Doug Vogt's information.

I remembered that the previous year, a friend of mine attended a workshop with David Wilcock. Jon came back from this several-day event talking about a solar flash as the sort of thing that could knock out the electrical grid. I listened to what he was saying, but decided Wilcock was off on a tangent and talking dramatic nonsense. The idea of the sun becoming explosive was the silliest thing I'd ever heard. I had long been aware of the possibility that another Carrington Event[94] could destroy our

---

94 The Carrington Event of 1859 was a powerful geomagnetic solar storm that knocked out telegraph wires and even started fires in telegraph offices.

power grid, and I thought the solar flash Wilcock was talking about was probably a large EMP. I listened politely, but ignored the subject. Now I wished I had been at Wilcock's workshop to hear what he had to say.

While in my library, I went back to look at Zecharia Sitchin's book, *The Twelfh Planet*, once again. I read it years earlier and was not impressed with his translation of Sumerican clay tablets, but I remembered the account of the Sumerian description of the Great Deluge. Here is the ancient text:

> "…the Moon disappeared…
> The appearance of the weather changed;
> The rains roared in the clouds…
> The winds became savage…
> …the Deluge set out,
> Its might came upon the people like a battle;
> One person did not see another,
> They were not recognizable in the destruction.
> The Deluge bellowed like a bull;
> The winds whinnied like a wild ass.
> The darkness was dense;
> The Sun could not be seen."

> The next translation was from *The Epic of Gilgamesh*:
> "With the glow of dawn
> a black cloud arose from the horizon:
> inside it, the god of storms thundered…
> Everything that had been bright
> turned to blackness…
> For one day the south storm blew,
> gathering speed as it blew,
> submerging the mountains…
> six days and six nights blows the wind
> as the South Storm sweeps the land.
> When the seventh day arrived,
> the Deluge of the South Storm subsided."

Putting this description next to Doug Vogt's description of the sun's micro-nova, it was obvious that the ancient texts were describing the events experienced in the nova cycle.

In rereading the section taken from Sumerian clay tablets, I noted that *the gods* knew the destruction was coming and did not tell the humans. How did the gods know? Was there an advanced civilization on the planet at that time, one with technology that could forecast the events and cycles of the stars and help them get away to safety? The gods were hoping that the humans would be destroyed. Retreating to an off-planet refuge, they watched the entire disaster unfold.

Here we were, thousands of years later, in almost the same situation. The elites of our time knew, and they hid that information. I was only guessing, but it looked to me like the Cabal had been building underground tunnels and cities that would protect them from the incinerating heat, the 200mph winds, the pulverizing debris, and the rampaging oceans moving across the continents. They spent decades developing new forms of energy that were not based on fossil fuels. They built technologies and transportation that gave them off-planet capacities designed to give them a better chance of survival if they could get to the back side of the planet or the moon where there was less chance of the debris storm hitting them. Stories circulated among today's people that the Cabal was planning something that would reduce population by more than half, and perhaps as much as 90%, if the Georgia Guidestones were any indication. No one knew exactly where that story was coming from, but quite a few people were paranoid about this aspect of Cabal intentions. Maybe they weren't planning to get rid of us as much as they were trying to save themselves, letting the sun's nova do the job of wiping out most of the population.

I remembered doing some research while working on Vol. 3 and coming across an essay in the *Nag Hamadi Scriptures* titled, "The Revelations of Adam." In the essay, Adam tells his son, Seth, that many people worship the god of fools, Sakla, and whenever a divine being comes to this Earth from the eternal Realms, the god Sakla creates "natural catastrophes in the hope of destroying those who came from the seed of life and gnosis." The natural disaster consisted of a "flood and destruction by fire, sulfur, and asphalt." The text went on to say that this occurs during "the eschatological struggle between opposing forces." Eschatology was the study of the end times. I thought that was a good description of where we were at in our world.

I also recalled a visit I'd had from several people a couple of years earlier. They were interested in plasma and wanted to talk about the subject. They brought me a copy of a paper by Dr. Anthony Peratt. The paper was titled, *Characteristics for the Occurrence of a High-Current, Z-pinch Aurora as Recorded in Antiquity.* It contained fascinating information about the shapes that high energy plasma takes during discharge, when unstable, or when involved in various energy transactions. What Peratt showed in this paper was how experiments done with plasma revealed shapes that perfectly matched ancient petroglyphs carved in rock around the world. My visitors and I talked about this, wondering if the ancient people knew about plasma, but I hadn't even come close to realizing the significance of this.

I went back to look at the paper and the photos in the paper and was impressed anew. How had the ancient people known about plasma physics? The only answer was that they observed plasma discharges directly in the skies above them.

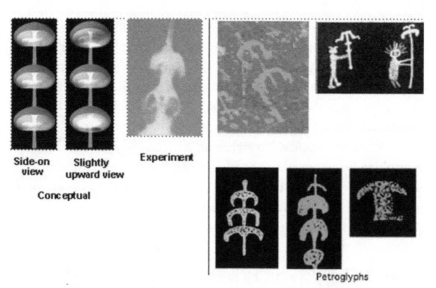

Side-on view   Slightly upward view   Experiment

Conceptual

Petroglyphs

Cupular formations from *Characteristics for the Occurrence of a High-Current, Z-pinch Aurora as Recorded in Antiquity* by Anthony Peratt.

Since ancient peoples knew everything was alive and conscious, their drawings often had a humanistic quality and looked like humans or animals. As I looked through Peratt's paper again, it was clear that the ancient peoples had to have witnessed a global phenomenon because the petroglyphs had been found in over eighty countries and states around the world.

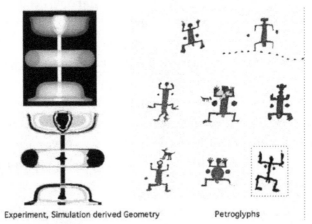

Experiment, Simulation derived Geometry   Petroglyphs

"Squatter man" shapes formed by the highest energy plasma releases known. From *Characteristics for the Occurrence of a High-Current, Z-pinch Aurora as Recorded in Antiquity* by Anthony Peratt.

There was never just one petroglyph in a given location. Sometimes thousands of them would be found in one area, many depicting various aspects of high-energy plasma. A familiar figure among the petroglyphs was known as the "Squatter" man. Most researchers dismissed this figure as just a depiction of early man dancing or celebrating. However, it closely matched the form taken by plasma during the highest energy plasma releases known to science. No archeologist or petroglyph researcher had been able to figure out why the two dots had been included, one on each side of the dancing figure until Peratt's work. Even the figure of Kokopelli, long known in the American southwest as a lyrical figure playing a flute was an effort to convey the end stage of a plasma discharge.

"They wouldn't have bothered to record all this if they weren't extremely impressed and trying to tell us something," I said to myself. Perhaps they had experienced the sun's nova cycle and were trying to warn us of what they had witnessed and feared might come again. Maybe they had laughed at the whole idea until it was too late, their civilization was destroyed, and all they had left to put messages on was rock walls.

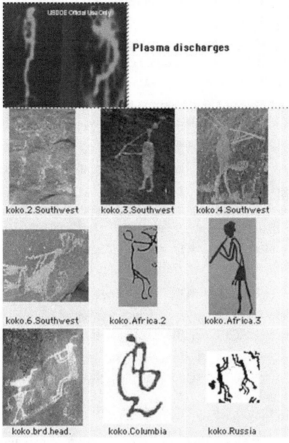

Shapes formed at the beginning and end of plasma discharge. From *Characteristics for the Occurrence of a High-Current, Z-Pinch Aurora as Recorded in Antiquity* by Anthony Peratt.

❧

For weeks after discovering the news about the nova cycle and the impending upending of our civilization, I was in a state of deep anxiety. The more I failed to find valid rebuttals to Vogt's work, the more anxious I became. It was as if a doctor had informed me that I had some terrible disease with only a year left to live. Within a few weeks I recognized that I was going through the five stages of grief—denial, anger, bargaining, depression, and acceptance.

First I tried to deny it. There must be a mistake, the people telling us that this is going to happen are wrong. Unable to think about anything else, I went looking for information that might contradict what he was saying, however, I kept finding further support for what Vogt was presenting. SuspiciousObservers.org was in the midst of creating an entire series titled *Earth's Catastrophe Cycle*. I watched it and was further discouraged about our future. Ben Davidson even brought in the subject of Peratt's work, coming to the same conclusion I had, that it was a heads-up warning from the past. MiasNewGlasses was another website talking about the whole disaster scenario.

I went back and yet again watched many of the videos by Doug Vogt, hoping to discover a major flaw in his reasoning process, but there was nothing of consequence. I went looking for other information or scientists that had another perspective. But all I found was more corroborating information. Other people were picking up on Vogt's work and adding to it. The pieces of truth just kept coming together.

Then came anger. Why hadn't the government told us about this? Why hadn't we been given a chance to prepare? Why had the space program been canceled when full development of space travel might have allowed us to get off the planet and out of the solar system? Were they building all those underground tunnels and cities so they had a place to save themselves? Were they really planning to run and hide when the sun went crazy, leaving the rest of us to our fates?

The anger was followed by a brief period of bargaining. Maybe we could convince God or the gods to intervene. Maybe we could talk to the sun, the wind, the oceans and ask them to do something different, something that wouldn't wipe out everyone and everything. I had a long-standing relationship with the sun, so I decided to have a conversation and ask it to skip its next nova. I was outside and had just finished feeding my chickens when I stopped to look up through the damp, frosty air at the sun.

"Hello, my friend," I said, speaking telepathically to the giant ball of light that I had often spoken with.

After a minute, there came a response, "Good day!"

"Friend, I need a special favor from you," I ventured.

"What is that?" the sun asked.

"Is it true that you blow off dust and debris every 12,000 years in something we humans call a nova cycle?" I said.

"That is correct," said the sun.

"Well...could I ask you to *not* do that...? I was feeling uncertain about making such a request.

"Are you asking me to not take care of myself when that is the very thing you teach the most?" the sun queried.

"Oh...well...no, I know you have to take care of yourself...but could you wait to do that until I'm no longer here on the planet? Maybe you could wait until I'm dead and gone?"

There was a pause. "Are you saying you want the nova cycle to happen to your children and grandchildren?" the sun asked in a very quiet way.

"Oh no! I don't want *that*...that's not what I'm trying to say. I'm trying to say that the whole nova cycle thing scares me and I don't know what to do!" I was definitely feeling anxious again.

The sun responded with one word in a long, drawn out command, *"Prepaa-a-a-re!"*

And then there was silence.

"But how? What should we do?" I half-questioned, half-demanded. There was no answer, only more silence. The connection was broken. I had no idea how to prepare.

I went in the house taking my eggs and the sun's one word of advice. I was upset with the advice because I had no idea how to prepare for such an event. In my mind, there was no way to prepare for 2000° temperatures, oceans moving across the land, or the obliteration of the sun by dust for years.

It was at that point I realized I was trying to bargain with the Universe. The failure to secure a successful bargain led to a feeling of helplessness and the result was a move into the next stage—depression. I couldn't think of anything else and couldn't focus on anything either.

Nothing was important, and all of the people, news, and conversations going on around me seemed trite and meaningless.

"What's the point...?" I asked myself over and over as I painted the hallways and discussed getting furniture re-upholstered. I felt scattered, lost, frightened, and so incredibly sad. I wanted to cry and couldn't. I wouldn't let myself, because I felt I might never quit. There was no hope. I was unable to put two coherent thoughts together. It looked like the end of the world to me. &

13 ∂

The Devils of War and the Deep Blue Sea

IF I THOUGHT I HAD THINGS TO WORRY ABOUT REGARDING TRUMP AND THE government, the information about the sun and it's regularly occurring micro-nova made the challenges coming from Trump, the sting, and our nation look pale by comparison. I felt I had nowhere to run or hide.

As if trying to match the uproar in myself, the situation in our country was getting more and more chaotic. It was just over a year since I'd put out the initial essay about Trump. I had received many requests for a sequel to *Trump and The Sting.* Maybe a sequel would help me organize the new information I had and renew my clarity about what was going on and what to do. It might be helpful for others as well. I started writing.

I had been working on the sequel for a couple of weeks when I happened to wonder what Gordon Duff thought of the whole Q movement. I knew he didn't like Trump, but he didn't ever seem to like anyone. Besides, I wasn't looking for yes-men or people who only agreed with my own point of view. I liked reading and having to digest the perspectives, ideas, and arguments on all sides of a situation because it helped me see the value and power of truth, recognize the foolishness of some, and find a perspective that was based in common sense.

Duff was cynical and direct and one of the sources I read from time to time because he had a lot of contacts around the world. He also had a totally different perspective and was often correct in his assessment of situations. I should have reminded myself of this before I went to the *VeteransToday.com* website where I read his latest post. By the time I finished reading, I was thoroughly dismayed and uncertain of what or who to believe.[90]

Duff said that there was no Deep State and that it was a fake term. He said Donald Trump was a member of the elites, that he was in bed with China, and that he was working to deliver the U.S. to China. The article was so convincing that I was completely undone. Trump, the man I had been watching and putting my trust in for the last two years, the one I hoped would deliver us from the staggering amount of corruption we were dealing with, was looking like a very good actor and nothing more.

"What am I supporting?" I asked myself. "Is it Donald Trump... or the illusion that we can go back to some version of life in these United States that I once knew? Is it Trump...or the foolish hope of regaining my own lost innocence and youth? Is it Trump...or the security of a fair and ethical society? Have I been a fool to believe in the goodness of the men and women in the Trump camp? A naïve idiot?"

I put away my writing and went to bed, thoroughly discouraged with everything—the world, the government, our nation, Donald Trump, Gordon Duff, my life, and our future. I was back to worrying that it was all a game and we were being played for suckers while the whole country was being pushed over some invisible edge from which there could be no return.

⁖

The next day, in a very somber mood, I was outside feeding the chickens and Agnes, my cow, when I heard a voice in my head as if someone were talking to me.

"Why are you shocked that Trump might be part of the Deep State? Is it possible that he has the old understanding long held by the

---

90 Duff, Gordon. *Intel Drop, March 10, 2016.* Veterans Today, 10 Mar 2019. https://www.veteranstoday.com/2019/03/10/intel-drop-march-10-2016/

European aristocracy that the peasants must also have a good life of their own making, their own choosing, or there will be trouble for all?

"Has it occurred to you that when he was approached by the military and asked to run for president, that he didn't just say yes? The man likes to make deals. Maybe he thought about this long and deeply, and did what is natural for him—he made a deal with the military.

"Now if you bring together a potential deal between Donald Trump and the military, what do you think the deal would consist of? Donald Trump is going to be interested in setting up a world where business and consumers thrive in spectacular fashion so they can buy things being produced and visit his casinos. He is going to want to create rules that favor and foster business around the world.

"On the other side, the military is going to be interested in getting the best weapons and the broadest permissions to use their power where they see fit. Since many of the military are very Christian, they wanted someone to play president while they took down the drug trafficking, sex trafficking, pedophilia rings, and child sacrifice rituals performed by Satanists.

"From the perspective of both Trump and the military, the common man is critically necessary because he is both laborer and consumer, making and selling things that provide the profit from which the elite businessman takes a bite. The common people are also the supplier of soldiers needed to operate the weapons and fight as directed.

"Why would you think Trump would suddenly abandon his old lifestyle or his former perceptions, information, and connections to go off and try to think like the masses? He is unique and special because he does *not* think like the masses. Wouldn't it be more realistic if, rather than abandon being an elite, he did exactly as you teach and simply *expanded* his sphere of thinking and action to take you and the rest of the masses into account, working to accomplish a world that works for all?

"Expecting Trump to suddenly join the masses and think like you think, act in the ways you act, and feel what you feel would be to lose the power he brings to the table. It would be the same as asking him to become your grandmother and raise fourteen children, while asking your grandmother to step into Trump's shoes and run the United States. Neither could do it. Neither would have the interest, the background, the experience, the language, or the gifts of the other. Has it occurred to you that you would have to let your grandmother be your grandmother and let Trump be Trump?

"Is it possible that you are just now seeing the work he is doing and other levels of action that you have not been privy to before now? Is it possible that your Gordon Duff is somewhat cynical because it keeps him from being caught up in wishful illusions like most of the population? Is most of your shock due to the dismay created by Duff's cynicism, and the rest of it due to the need to expand your thinking to recognize that you were thinking in terms of a single track in which you and the rest of the masses were the beneficiary, whereas Trump is operating in a multi-track environment in which presidents, kings, and millionaires also benefit? Were you expecting Trump to come over to your "side" and abandon his "side?" Were you thinking that Trump should not be Trump?

"Go back and read Gordon Duff's article again and try to see beyond the words. When you are finished reading, remember this...You cannot move to the next level of consciousness if you are not thinking in terms of multi-dimensional service to a multi-layered existence."

I came inside, hung up my coat, put away the eggs, and immediately wrote down what I had heard. It helped. I was not as glum.

Later in the day, I sat with a cup of tea thinking about our situation in the U.S. If we were not being suckered, and all of this was not a game, what was it? There was only one answer that fit. It was a war.

If it was a war...and if the Deep State was a fake term...and if Gordon Duff was right in saying that all gambling and "hospitality" includes human trafficking...and if Donald Trump was in the hospitality business, a working member of the elites whose network of hotels and casinos were involved in sex, drugs, and gambling...and if sex, drugs, gambling, *and* human trafficking were used as payoffs in all banking and big, multi-national, corporate businesses on the planet...then there must have been a deep split among the corporate-banking behemoths, a serious disagreement that sparked this war...and what we were seeing was a fight between the most powerful men on the planet and their corporations....a war to control men, money, militaries, and the minds of entire nations...a war that would settle the question of who would control the trillions of dollars in hidden gold that would back those who could make it to the top...a war between the sneaky Cabal side and the self-righteous Christian military side...a war to rule the world.

If it was a war, then mainstream media's continuous hammering of Donald Trump as the figurehead on the Christian military side was understandable. This was something that went on in all wars. They were using psychological tactics to drum up support for their side and create discouragement on the side of their enemies.

If it was a war, what if the Q information was no different from the mainstream media effort—a highly sophisticated psychological operation designed to build support for the Christian side of the war without revealing too much about either side of the elite factions or their real goals?

If it was a war, and we were only seeing twenty percent of the fighting, as Q had said, was it because the remaining eighty percent of the fighting was in areas that *both* sides wanted to keep hidden so that certain structures and advantages would be there for them if they won?

Suddenly everything in my consciousness tilted. The idea of good guys vs. bad guys struck me as overly simplistic, even childish. How silly of me to think Trump was fighting to make all *my* expectations come true. What if the war had nothing to do with rescuing the American people from the Cabal? What if it had very little to do with restoring the Constitution and the rule of law or making American great again? I didn't *think* this was the case, but I had no proof other than the carrot of hope held out there by QAnon.

Was the real goal to maintain elite power one way or the other? Were our hopes being whipped up into believing that something was being done to reduce corruption so that we would cooperate and work as cheer- leaders during the fight? Were we being kept occupied and only informed about 20% of the battle because we might revolt altogether if we knew the truth about the other 80%? Did both sides want to keep it hidden because neither side wanted us to know how enslaved we were? Did they not want us to see the hidden structures of power or grasp how the world of the super-rich operated? Did they not want us to realize how much money was at their disposal when we were all so poor and working so hard to fill basic needs? Were they trying to hide how irrelevant our national government was and that it had only been left in place to keep us thinking that we had any power?

I held the idea of two warring factions of elites at arm's length and considered this with a more appraising eye. One faction was based in Satanism as a source of power and righteousness, while the other faction was based in Christianity as their source of power and righteousness. If Gorden Duff was correct, both sides were anchored in massive networks of sex, drugs, alcohol, gambling, and entertainment. However, it looked like one side (the Cabal) was also engaged in sorcery, human sacrifice, slavery, and other sordid activities like organ harvesting and adrenochrome supply, while the Christian side fancied itself to be cleaner, of a higher caliber, more classy, and even more honest in their approach to handling the business of sex, drugs, alcohol, and gambling. They were both fighting for total control of the planet, and probably, each was justifying their way of doing things.

If there was a deal between Trump and the military, what was it? The military was heavily Christian and might have wanted to end what they saw as overwhelming sin in the form of murder, theft, sex trafficking, pedophilia, financial fraud, and other horrors. Trump may have been running into territorial problems in places where he wanted to open hotels or casinos where the Cabal had control. He may have been frustrated by the stupidity of the Cabal in gutting countries financially just because they could, which left every impoverished and without enough money. He may have disagreed with their plans to set up an entirely new governmental system that suited them with an economy that was completely controlled and took away some of the fun he experienced in the 'art of the deal.' He may have had a personal distaste for the kinds of pedophilia, child sacrifice, and organ trafficking that he saw becoming common among the Satanists and decided he had to do something about it. Trump may even have had a personal penchant for beauty, order, and success that was shared with the public. He may have developed a deep love for his children and wanted a secure life for them. The fact is, we do not know what his motives were. All we know is that he and the military made a deal in which Trump would be president and the military would not have to carry out a coup d'etat. Each could pursue their own goals by working together.

Something in me had shifted at a deep level. I was no longer seeing Trump as just the man who would end corruption and return us to a more civilized, less corrupt life. I liked that view, but it was no longer enough. Seeing the entire situation as a war was one shift. I recalled Q having commented that "this is war," but that fact hadn't sunk in and I continued to view it as more of a game for many months. Seeing the war from a more distanced perspective was another shift. It felt as if whatever the billionaires were doing in their fight up there at the top was of no relevance to those of us at the bottom. I knew in my head that this wasn't true, that their fights were relevant to all of us, but I was back to feeling helpless, feeling like there was little-to-nothing the common people could do. We still had to go to work, earn a living, and wash our socks.

Q had said that eventually Facebook, Amazon, Google, Twitter, and other big companies would be taken apart, but the implications of this had not been apparent until now. Those companies represented the corporate billionaires who were aligned against Trump /Christian side. Those companies were all on the side of, and run by, the Cabal. From the point of view of the Cabal, those were the institutions being used to manipulate the population and being taken apart would be tantamount to losing the war and the chance to rule the world—and all of that gold.

Suddenly, it was clear—not only was it a war, I was seeing the entire war as the clash of titanic corporations that would fight to the death, or at least dismemberment of their corporate bodies. On one side was Donald Trump and his team of nationalists that included more than a few hidden billionaires. On the other side were the opposing billionaires—Jeff Bezos, Mark Zuckerberg, Eric Schmidt, Jack Dorsey, Carlos Slim, and of course, the Rothschild-Soros-Saudi group. It looked to me like a David and Goliath sort of battle. Bezos was the head of Amazon and also owned the Washington Post, Zuckerberg headed Facebook, Schmidt had stepped down but was still very much in play regarding Google, Dorsey was head of Twitter, and Slim was the major owner of the New York Times. This did not even begin to take into account the pharmaceuticals, chemical giants, insurance companies, universities, or foreign heads of state that were owned and run by the Rothschild-Soros-Saudi group who were in favor of globalism, socialism, and the New World Order.

I remembered something the Robes had said many years earlier. "With control over huge amounts of wealth, their own spies, teams of lawyers and legal analysts, communication networks and expanded customer service centers, armed security and even assassins, they will hope to step seamlessly into the position vacated by governments, dropping any corporate structures that belong to the old ways or do not make money, and picking up as much power as they can."

In 1980, the Robes had said the big corporations would run things for between thirty and fifty years. When I asked, "When will that begin?" they responded saying "It has already begun." It had now been 40 years since their comment. They had gone on to say that in the struggle to claim, "I rule the world!!" the big corporations would end up taking one another down through a series of betrayals, disinformation, and insider battles. Suddenly, it looked like that was exactly what we were witnessing!

In some ways, not to glorify the elites in any way, the war between the two factions appeared to be almost like a dramatization of struggles between the gods taking place so far above us that we the people were mostly distant onlookers and just needed to stay out of the way. We were the supporters in the peanut gallery who provided support, encouragement, and applause for our favorite side. We were the audience and needed to recognize that the fight was not really about us. It was even questionable as to whether or not it was *for* us. In many ways it had little to do with us other than the observation that we were once again pawns, used by the Cabal as chattel, or by the Christians as consumers who worked to fill their coffers. Maybe it had nothing to do with us other than that it was forcing us to wake up to the fact that the days of nations were probably numbered, the rise of business to power was nearing its climax, and we were moving into an unknown future that was looking more and more uncertain.

This perception deepened when the Cathedral of Notre Dame was destroyed by fire, and a few days later there was a retaliatory attack on Christian churches and hotels in Sri Lanka. At first, I thought the Notre Dame cathedral became a casualty because it was on the Christian side of the war and the Cabal had taken it out using fire. But it turned out that the catacombs under Notre Dame were being used by the Cabal for human sacrifice rituals. It was the Christians who took it out. They burned down one of their own edifices on Good Friday to prevent the sacrifice ritual that was scheduled for Easter Weekend. In a retaliation that demonstrated the global nature of the war, the Cabal attacked Christian churches in Sri Lanka.

We were two years into Trump's presidency and, for those who were tracking QAnon and watching what was going on behind the scenes, we were sixteen months into the war. Each of us watching the unfolding drama from the sidelines wanted to see our version of the bad guys go down and the good guys win.

Over the centuries, there had been lots of wars, lots of winners and losers, but things seldom worked out the way anyone thought it would. Perpetrators of war often went to their grave early because life was short, because they made stupid choices, or because they wore themselves out taking huge risks and creating disastrous or stressful situations that they then got caught up in. Stress was a killer just as surely as bullets and laser beams.

Until Easter weekend, it had looked to me like a long coup was being countered by a sting. Now the idea of a coup or a sting was almost too limiting. We were dealing with a war. Was the Trump team going to win the war? If they won, would they continue to hold the attitude of the old European monarchs that believed the peasants needed to have a reasonably good life or there would be trouble in the kingdom? There was no way to predict anything with certainty.

What if we got the whole national vs. globalist government argument ironed out only to have the entire civilization wiped out by the sun's nova? Was it worth fighting for the nation and trying to make

America great again? We were doing what made sense, given the bigger picture?

I wasn't sure about anything any more. It was late at night. I was tired. The whole situation was too overwhelming, too dramatic, like something out of the movies. My perception that somebody was actually standing up and doing something had changed drastically to the perception that we were all pawns in a game of chess, watching two sides battle it out while trying to capture one another's kings but forgetting to watch the sidelines for unexpected black swans.

"How quickly security and confidence in the future can disappear," I thought as I got ready for bed. &

14 ❧

Journey to Another Earth

I WAS TRYING TO IGNORE MY FEELINGS WHEN A PHONE CALL CAME IN FROM the same friend who had attended the seminar given by David Wilcock the previous year, the one I had pooh-poohed and dismissed as silly. In the conversation, I was trying to sound reasonable and focused, but I felt like I was on the edge of hysteria, something that was extremely rare for me.

I don't recall what the entire conversation was about, but suddenly I was rattling on about the fact that I was not in a good frame of mind because of the coming micro-nova. I didn't think he understood the extent of what that meant, but I didn't care and proceeded to run on about intense heat, dust clouds, and oceans rolling across continents. Since Jon had attended David Wilcock's seminar earlier, he had some idea of what I was talking about, but he was thinking of the event as a solar flash that might destroy our electrical grid, while I was trying to correct that view by introducing him to the more expansive picture Doug Vogt was talking about. Somewhere in that conversation, he talked me down off the ledge.

One of the things I always appreciated about Jon was his level-headedness, his ability to stay calm under pressure, and his trust in his own ability to figure out a strategy that would get him out of trouble. Maybe it was a characteristic of many years of piloting airplanes when you quickly understand that the surest way to guarantee crashing to your death is to panic. I don't remember much of what he said, but somewhere in the course of the conversation he pointed out that Delores Cannon's work kept bringing up the idea of two earths and maybe it was referring to a possibility we hadn't considered.

"What are you saying!?" I snapped.

"I don't know!" he shot back. "You're the one with all of the experiences! You're the one who's traveled to other places! You tell me!!"

All at once, I was remembering something that happened in the early years of kundalini that I had never been able to figure out. It was actually a trio of events comprised of several journeys made when three beings of light invited me to go with them and took me to another world. At the time, I had no idea why those beings had come to me or why they asked me to go with them. In all the years since, I was never able to explain why I'd had those particular experiences nor could I relate those experiences to anything of value or significance in my everyday life. The result was that they just hung there in the back closet of my mind. Everything in my life was changing because of the kundalini, and the changes were continuous, deep, frightening, and difficult to deal with. I was struggling to maintain a façade of normalcy.

When kundalini awakens, consciousness awakens. When consciousness awakens, you are *awake* and sleep does not occur because consciousness has no need to sleep. Only the body needs to sleep, and consciousness, once fully awakened, is continuously awake regardless of what the body is doing. I did not sleep for three years even though I put myself to bed every night.

Each night, when my body began to relax in the bed, I would end up sliding out of it and then be uncertain of what to do with myself. Since I had never heard of metaphysics or out-of-body experiences and had no idea why this was happening, I would float up through the ceiling and end up sitting on the roof. There I sat through the night, watching the water in the bay, the animals in the field across the highway, the traffic on Jefferson Avenue, or the planes flying in and out of Selfridge Air Force base, which was just a half mile down the street from my home in Mt. Clemens, MI.

One night, I had been sitting on the roof for a while when I noticed three faint lights off in the distance. "Here comes another plane," I thought to myself, then gazed off in other directions absentmindedly.

A short time later, I wondered why I hadn't heard the sound of the incoming plane. I looked in the direction of the three lights. They were closer, but now they didn't quite look right. I wondered what kind of plane it was, and continued to watch until I realized it wasn't a plane at all. The three lights came closer and closer until they were directly above me and I saw that they were three beings of light, brilliant light! Two of them reached out their hands to me and said, "Come with us."

Not having anything else to do, I reached up to take their hands. They took off, pulling me along with them, and it was everything I could do to hang on. We were moving at a dizzying speed, I could see lights streaking by, and I felt like one of those Russian dolls that you open to find another doll, then another and another, with the body of each doll being shed and left behind, one after another, like stages of a rocket as we sped forward. I could barely open my eyes because the pressure of the acceleration was so great.

After what seemed like a long time and a great distance, we slowed down and in the distance I could see a ball of light. As we drew closer, I saw that it was a planet, and soon we were slowly descending toward its surface. As we did so, every pebble, blade of grass, leaf, flower, tree, building, brick, stone, and inhabitant was greeting me with overflowing love as if they all knew me personally and were welcoming home a beloved member of the family. This was remarkable enough in itself, but even more remarkable was the fact that I was aware of every single pebble, flower, and person on the planet, every building and brick—everything—as a personal friend.In this moment of reunion, we were all greeting one another as if we were intimate friends that had known each other forever and loved one another deeply. It is difficult to convey my joy at seeing them and being home again!

On the first of these visits, the three beings took me on a tour of one of the cities and I was dazzled by the exuberant beauty and sparkling cleanliness that was everywhere. The grace and friendliness of the people was extraordinary, and the fact that I knew everyone so well made me feel like I fit in perfectly.

However, the thing that was most unusual, the thing I had never been able to reconcile, was the fact that I recognized the place as Earth! Every detail of this unusual place was a duplicate of the same Earth I lived on every day, except that in this place there was no sickness, no war or anger, no hurt, sorrow, fighting, argument, or unhappiness of any kind. Everyone looked like normal humans, but no one was old, overweight, sick, disfigured, or depressed, and there was no trash or litter anywhere.

About a month later, the three beings of light came and got me again, taking me to the same place. On that visit, we went into the countryside where we walked through stunning gardens, fields of flowers and forests where numerous wild animals lived and interacted peacefully with us. I remember stopping to look into flowers made of light and watching their inner workings. I talked to birds and animals, and watched a gardener move a tree by communicating with it and asking it to move about 10 feet over, which it did by dissolving and then reassembling itself in the spot the gardener was pointing to!

I don't recall how much time elapsed between the second and third visits, I just remember the three beings coming to get me from the roof again, the incredible joy of the arrival, and one memorable incident. In this beautiful, joy-filled world, telepathy was the norm and everyone was aware of the thoughts and feelings of everyone and everything else. In the midst of this joy, someone, a relative newcomer, had a moment of intense frustration that was immediately picked up by every person, plant, and animal living there. Everyone instantly dropped what they were doing and turned their attention to the frustrated individual. A few gathered around him, filling him with silent love, encouragement, and healing light. They did not interrupt or interfere, but their focus did not waver or shift until, within a short time, the frustration was replaced by insight, understanding, and a return to inner peace. Everyone went back to whatever they had been doing, but each took a bit of deeper wisdom about how to quickly resolve that form of frustration after watching him resolve it in himself. I was amazed by this!

When the third visit was over, the beings of light told me I was welcome to stay, but I would have to give up all of the ideas I held about a reality system and how it should operate. I thought about my children and said I didn't think I could stay. They did not seem disappointed or upset at all. They simply smiled and said "You will be back." As I prepared to leave, they commented that we would all come to live there eventually. Then the three beings of light brought me back.

I did not think about the experiences very much after they happened because so many other unexplained things were going on in my consciousness at that time. However, once in a while I would remember it and wonder, "Why did I have those experiences? Why had the place looked like a duplicate of the Earth?" There were never any answers to those questions, so I went about my life, leaving the questions dangling.

Now here I was, forty years later, looking at those visits, thinking about the fact that I had visited a place that looked just like the Earth, putting that alongside Delores Cannon's work, and asking myself, "What am I seeing here? Was I literally on that Earth that Cannon's subjects were talking about? Is there another Earth?"

This line of thinking led to recall of another experience. This occured in 1980 when a group of little men in brown robes appeared and said they wanted to show me some pictures. When I finally agreed to cooperate, the first thing they did was take me far enough away from the Earth to be able to see the entire planet.

When I wrote about the experience in my earlier book, *Robes*, I didn't say much about the destruction I saw because it was too awful and I didn't want the book to be a doom-and-gloom book. I wanted readers to focus on the future and what we could create if we would develop our consciousness and then our world the way the Robes showed was possible.

The only part of the conversation I reported in Robes concerned the electromagnetic wave frequencies around the planet because I thought that was a fascinating aspect of the solar system. I left out other things I saw, things that occurred in the aftermath of the untethered Earth. The situation on the planet was not good. The global civilization was practically destroyed and the majority of those who survived the initial destruction slowly died out from starvation and the effects of radiation from hundreds of ruined nuclear plants that dotted the landscape, especially in North America and Western Europe. Water was everywhere but was unfit to drink. Trees were gone, taking their fruits and nuts with them. Agriculture was a thing of the past, and even hunting was difficult because so many animals had perished.

As time went by, I pushed the awful things I saw into the category of *highly unlikely...almost certainly impossible*. They ended up classified in my mind as distant, allegorical events that only happened in stories about other people in faraway times and places. Now I went back to read what I had written so long ago.

> I knew that my body was sitting on the floor in the living room of my house, but my entire perceptual and sensory system was standing with this group of little strangers out in space at the edge of the atmosphere, looking at a most beautiful planet, the Earth. It appeared like a volleyball that was somehow caught or suspended in a large, 3-dimensional volleyball net. The volleyball net was electrically charged and shimmered with a faint, pulsing glow.

> "...The first thing you should understand is that the Earth is a living being and is quite capable of healing herself. When she does, there can be a shift of many degrees, even a complete rolling over." Their words were accompanied by a slight tremor in the earth as we viewed it.

> "The net you are looking at is like a network of electromagnetic and other wave forces that move through space and intersect, as well as interact, with the waves— electromagnetic and otherwise—given off by Earth.

> "As these waves move through space, they strike the Earth from all directions, some holding the planet in place, some moving through or around her, causing a steady rotation. The axis Earth rotates around is the path energy takes as it

moves through the body of the planet, and of course, this creates your north and south poles..."

I did not know what to say at this point. I was still stuck on the very first thing they said, which was that the Earth was a living being. This sounded preposterous to me, and the idea that the Earth could shift its position in space seemed like an impossible fiction. When added to my already serious doubts about whether it was a good idea to watch their pictures, listen to their words and give the little men the courtesy of acting as if they were real, the information proved to be almost too much. My initial willingness to hear them out or to look at their pictures began shriveling.

I was about to protest or try to withdraw from the experience when the Earth and the volleyball net sort of shrugged. Bulging awkwardly like a pregnant woman in the last trimester, the Earth rolled forward, rolled back, bobbled around a bit, then resettled itself in an entirely new position. The oceans rolled and splashed like water in a bathtub and even from my distant vantage point, I could see considerable destruction as whole sections of land rose up and folded over on themselves, burying everyone and everything, leaving the surface as bare and new as the moon...The blank, empty surface areas in some places looked as though no one, human or animal, had ever lived there...

"You know," the little men interrupted my silence, "ongoing change on the part of Earth is to be expected, and the activities of humans will certainly either aggravate or ameliorate these changes. At the very least, you should be aware that these things have happened in the past and will continue to happen in the future. At best, your lifestyle could be much more fluid, more prepared to deal with such changes."

"Are you saying this could happen in my lifetime?" I asked, thinking that if it was going to happen far into the future, I needn't get upset or feel I had to do something different.

"If the Earth changes come in your lifetime and you are in the habit of expecting others to feed you, to provide the electricity that makes your homes livable and your appliances useful, to provide fresh water and fuel, and the knowledge of healing, then you are lost. Even very small changes in the Earth would require you to know how to provide these things for yourselves...Humankind needn't suffer at all if there could be a little more development of the human body/mind system."

—from *Robes - A Book of Coming Changes.*

As I read through what the Robes had said and shown me in that long-ago visit, I was surprised all over again by several things. One was their reference to the "network of electromagnetic and other wave forces that move through space." Back then, I found this information interesting, but now it struck me as amazing that they were talking about an electric universe, yet they gave this information at a time when the view of how things worked was still based on Newtonian physics.

As I read what I had written so many years earlier, I realized that I completely missed their suggestion that we "needn't suffer at all if there could be a little more development of the body/mind system." I had skipped over this statement about suffering because I was already denying what I had seen.

Since I hadn't taken the idea of the Earth rolling over or bobbing about in space seriously, I never considered the deeper implications of the comments that accompanied what they were showing me, nor had I paid proper attention to their suggestion regarding the need to develop consciousness. I observed what they were showing me, but was not really taking in what I was seeing, partly because it was so disturbing, and partly because my attention was caught up in their comment that "The Earth is a living being." The implications of this were that the Earth was alive, that it was aware, and that it was capable of healing itself, all of which were incredibly overwhelming ideas to me at that point in my life. I don't think

I had ever given the Earth a single thought prior to that moment, let alone considered it to be alive and aware.

There was nothing in my education or background that offered any validation or explanation for such weird potential behavior on the part of the planet, and I could not imagine why a planet would suddenly begin rolling about in space. This kind of movement was simply not realistic until I heard Doug Vogt's lectures.

Sadly, I had dismissed many of the scenes the Robes showed me as unlikely, impossible, and too awful to contemplate. I also failed to ask myself, "Why would the little men in brown robes show me such a scene?" Now, forty years later, that question hit like a thunderbolt! *Why* did they show me that scene of the Earth looking like a giant beachball floating on the waves of space as it rolled and bobbed about?! That was the very *first* thing they showed me. Why *that*? Were they trying to tell me something and I was too dense to understand or to ask what I was supposed to do with that information?

Now I read and reread their words. "...ongoing change on the part of Earth is to be expected, and the activities of humans will certainly either aggravate or ameliorate these changes. At the very least, you should be aware that these things have happened in the past and will continue to happen in the future. At best, your lifestyle could be much more fluid, more prepared to deal with such changes," they had said.

I was embarassed to admit that my response to this was to fuss about whether such changes would happen in my lifetime—or if I could safely ignore the whole warning and go on with life as usual.

"If the Earth changes come in your lifetime and you are in the habit of expecting others to feed you, to provide the electricity that makes your homes livable and your appliances useful, to provide fresh water and fuel, and the knowledge of healing, then you are lost. Even very small changes in the Earth would require you to know how to provide these things for yourself. If the changes come in the lives of your children, then *they* are lost, for you would not have taught them what they needed to know to survive in the face of changes that might require fending for one's self.

"If the changes come in the lives of your grandchildren and great-grandchildren, then *you* are lost again, for by that time you will have returned to a new life on Earth, for another round of lessons in soul development, and will suffer your own consequences anyway."

Then they pointed out something that I had completely forgotten about.

"Humankind needn't suffer at all if there could be a little more development of the human body/mind."

Exactly what did they mean by that? I had developed a little bit of understanding and skill with consciousness, but what they were hinting at was beyond where I was at or had even thought of going.

Finally, I began to pull myself together. Things had happened in my own life that I had never been able to figure out. Now they were beginning to come together—unexpectedly and in a way they never had before. &

15 ❧

Sky Problems and Confrontations

IT CAN TAKE A VERY LONG TIME TO PUT ALL THE PIECES TOGETHER TO MAKE sense of your life. In doing so, the meaning of some events can shift dramatically. "You will have to put it all together for yourself once I am gone," said Don Juan, one of my best teachers. Suddenly I was putting all sorts of pieces together.

I had long wondered about something I'd heard at a meeting that took place in the conference room of Dr. Wm. Levengood. A group of us had gathered there on a Sunday afternoon. I can't recall the year or even exactly what the reason was for the meeting, but I think it had something to do with ETs, abductions, and the energy changes that occurred in connection with them. Levengood found that whether you were dealing with UFO landing sites, animal mutilations, or actual abductions, an energetic fingerprint was left behind, enabling us to detect the presence of ET beings and their spacecraft because they had much higher energies than what was normally found in the general human environment. This energetic fingerprint affected the plasma energy of whatever was exposed to it whether that was leaves, soil, water, stones, equipment, clothing, plants, animals, or humans. At any rate, there were about 15 or 20 people attending the meeting and the conversation flowed back and forth as they shared their stories and experiences. A woman named Landi Hurd shared something I never forgot.

She told us that she had been abducted from time to time since she was a little girl. However, she was a grown woman with husband and children when she had a curious experience. She was asleep one night when something woke her. She said she had an overwhelming urge to go downstairs and open the front door. She finally got up and went down the stairs to the door, and when she opened it, there on the porch was a tall Nordic-looking being and a couple of shorter grey beings. She was taken on board a craft and taken to a place that looked like the Earth, except that the colors were almost "see-through."

She said she noticed something was going on with the sky and this distracted her. She asked the ETs what was wrong with the sky because it looked extremely disturbed and as if something terrible was happening.

I don't recall whether or not they answered her question. Instead they said something along the lines of, "There will come a time in the future when we will come to you, ask you to go with us, and you will have only a couple of seconds to say yes or no. There will not be time to pack a suitcase, say goodbye to husbands, children, or anyone else. If you say yes, you will leave with us immediately. We will return you later, when it is safe to do so. We tell you this now so you will have time to decide." With that, they took her back. She said she felt that whatever was going on with the sky was the reason they were giving her the warning and that it must have been something catastrophic.[95]

When I heard her tell this story, I asked what on earth she thought was going on with the sky. She commented that it almost looked like the sky was on fire, and that it certainly didn't look normal.

As I thought about this after the meeting, I had all sorts of questions. Why were the ETs concerned for her safety? What was her connection to them? What did they know about astronomy, the Earth, or the sky that we were not aware of but probably needed to know? Why would they have only seconds to pick her up? Where were they going to go in such a

---

95 See Landi's book, *Beyond the Sky: A Lifetime of Alien Contact.*

hurry? Why were things going to be unsafe here for a while? There were no answers to these questions back then, but now I found myself thinking it might have been because of the disasters triggered by the nova cycle.

As I was thinking about Landi's story, I remembered one of my own encounters with ETs. I wrote about this encounter in *Consciousness and Energy, Vol. 2* and described the rather difficult meeting in some detail. I recount it here for those who have not read Volume 2:

> During my last visit, however, things had gone a little differently. I was picked up and brought before the same group of beings. They again questioned me as to what I had done to move in the direction of the work I had agreed to do. I told them I had built a learning center and was working to develop the consciousness of those humans who were interested in evolving and building a new world. In truth, I had only gone along with building the learning center because it was something I thought Jim wanted to do, but I left that little detail to the background and presented it as if it was my idea. Besides, the learning center had been a useful place to write and teach, which also allowed me to make a living.

> Once again, the beings just looked at me. Finally, one of them spoke up.

> "It is too late. The Earth cannot be saved. It does not deserve to be saved. You are about to self-destruct and there is nothing we can do about it. There is nothing we wish to do about it. Such a destructive species should be allowed to collapse. It is too bad. It is such a unique world system. We were certain you would recognize how unique and precious it is, but not enough of you care to take action."

> "Then why did you pick me up and bring me here?" I asked, suddenly aware of my teacher, Makumrakh, and the night the greenhouse lit up in the darkness of the back yard.

> "Because we wanted to inform you as a member of the team that it was too late," he replied.

"I don't think it's too late," I said in a stubbornly conversational tone.

"What do you base that on?" he inquired.

"We're just getting started," I said.

"You're starting too late," he reiterated, "and the type of life system you have on earth cannot suffer so many insults."

"What type of life system are you talking about?" I asked, thinking he was referring to humans and that, in my mind, we were actually doing just fine.

"An integrative system," he replied.

I had to stop and think about that for a moment. I knew what integrative meant, but at that moment I could not quite get my mind around the full scope of what he was saying. Finally, I simply repeated what I had already said, "I don't think it's too late."

"It is too late," he said.

Suddenly I was uneasy and afraid that I was, indeed, guilty of not doing what I had come here to do. This was followed by a rising tide of frustration with the entire Earth reality system and the stubborn, fearful ignorance of the people who lived there. Why were we even trying to save them? At the same time, I became aware of how much I had come to love the entire place, from the smallest bug to the tallest mountain, from the newborn children to the stout-hearted adults who were doing their best to raise those children even though they didn't have a clue what they were doing. These people needed time...time to make changes and a new view of the space they inhabited. How dare these righteous-sounding beings who weren't even living in this reality system tell me that it was too late!

Completely unwilling to accept his pronouncement of "too late," I loudly blurted out, "What do you mean, 'it's too late?'

How can it be too late? We're still eating and drinking and breathing and having babies! We're still working our asses off every day! We're still trying to deal with a totally corrupt government! We're still trying to save dolphins and baby seals! Don't we get credit for any of this? Yes, we're moving slowly because we're still trying figure out who to listen to and what action to take that won't get us killed or set us back even further, so don't tell me it's too late! In fact, it's NOT too late!" I was getting quite worked up.

The beings looked at me calmly and said, "Too many systems are in full decline. Your civilization is going to collapse and the evolutionary step that was so close will not be taken. You will return to primitive man status. It is too late to save you."

By this time, I was getting angry. They seemed to want to give up before we gave up. "It is not too late!" I shouted at them.

"What makes you think it is not too late?" the leader of the group asked in a slightly louder voice that was ever so polite yet held a faint touch of disdain for my show of anger. I knew they did not like anger and considered it evidence of a lack of self-control, but by now I didn't care.

"Because I have raised TEENAGERS!" I roared, my arms waving wildly as if to emphasize my words. "I KNOW what it is like to think it is hopeless! I know how to believe in someone and to hold a space of love and possibility for them until they can step in and hold that space for themselves! You can't give up, and I am not giving up. Yes, it is late and there may be some pain, but it is not TOO late! We are just getting STARTED. If you thought we were worth saving before, don't give up just because it is too late for some. We will need your help because it is not too late!"

There was total silence in the room. I stood bug-eyed and defiant, daring them to contradict me. No one moved for what seemed like an eternity. And then the leader made a barely discernible nod. I was led to another room where another meeting was held."

As I reviewed the encounter, I was seeing it with completely new eyes. I had argued with their observation that we were about to self-destruct. They said that such a destructive species should be allowed to collapse, a statement that still stung.

My reaction after all this time was still defensive. "It's not our fault that the sun regularly goes through a nova cycle, creating chaos and destruction," I thought. Then, right on the heels of this thought came a moment when the light went on in my mind. "What if they were pointing out that the development of consciousness and an evolutionary leap could have affected the outcome of the entire proecess if we had only done the work we needed to do? What if to fail to raise and expand consciousness was tantamount to suicide because we would be unable to shift into a consciousness that allowed us to navigate the destruction...or possibly move to a New Earth similar to the one the three beings of light had taken me to?"

There was a concept in science called *superposition*. Superposition postulated that the Earth existed in all possible states. If we had developed our consciousness, could we have moved to a version of Earth where the nova cycle did not occur?

When I told the ETs I had built a learning center and was working to develop the consciousness of those who were interested in evolving themselves and building a new world, I was thinking that the evolution of consciousness would convince us to stop poisoning our food and water. I thought it would convince us to stop buying things that only lasted for one use and then went to the landfill; to stop spraying the skies, the fields, and the lawns with terrible chemicals; and to stop working at jobs that did not feed the soul or nurture creativity, joy, and consciousness. I thought a more awakened consciousness would help relieve some of the anger people were feeling, get us to start taking better care of the body, be more present and compassionate, and a thousand other things that would make our world more tolerable.

Back then, I thought their comments referred to the need to become more sustainable, and to me, sustainability meant clean air, clean water, and less trash. When the ETs stated that we 'were starting too late... and the type of life system we have on earth could not suffer so many insults,' I assumed they were talking about a better life for humans, plants, and animals. But what if the sustainability they were talking about meant getting us to develop consciousness enough to sustain ourselves in the face of great natural disasters? What if a collapse of civilization was going to occur because of the ravages of the nova cycle and not because we had dirty air, too much trash, or were spraying too many poisons? What if they were talking about survival in the face of planetary and solar system changes?

I remembered the little men in brown robes telling me that they definitely wanted us to survive. I also recalled their insistence that the only unavoidable thing in life was the development of consciousness. At the time, I had not connected these two statements the way I was connecting them now.

Back then, I had not grasped what the ETs meant when they said our world was an integrative system. I knew what the word meant; I just couldn't apply it to the planet at that minute. The definition of *integrate* is "to combine one thing with another so that they become a whole; to bring into equal participation in a group or institution." What if the ETs meant that the entire reality system of sun, oceans, planet, humans, plants and animals was one, single entity, having one integrated base of consciousness? If that was the case, then any one of the forms of consciousness within the system could impact the consciousness of the whole system.

I had failed to understand the meaning of the statement that all systems were in full decline. This would include the sun, the Earth's rotation, and the magnetic forces that kept us stable. Did their comment refer only to the physical systems, or did it also indicate that the entire reality system of plant, animal, human, and planetary consciousness was going to implode because it had not evolved to some point of power that could have been reached if we had developed a little further? What if the ETs were trying to say that in an integrative system, the participants—whoever or whatever they might be—had the opportunity, even the obligation, to move the entire system up a notch, preventing destruction and earning a chance to continue living and evolving within a reality system of their choosing. Was that what they meant by "an evolutionary leap?"

In my musings about coming to love the entire place, from the smallest bug to the tallest mountain, from the newborn children to the stout-hearted adults doing their best to raise those children, I had admitted that people needed time to make changes and develop a new view of the space they inhabited. I thought we had lifetimes to make the change, and that I could help get it started. But what if they insisted that it was too late was because there was a deadline—the coming nova? Was their insistence that it was too late based on knowledge of that disaster and an understanding of how long it takes to actually shift consciousness and then stabilize it? What if the "evolutionary step that was so close" was the step into a permanently altered state of consciousness that held great power? I had stepped into that kind of consciousness more than once, and I knew the kind of time and training that such a step would require.

I thought about the planet herself, wondering if she was afraid. It was one thing if the people on the planet were being destructive to the planet, but few thought about the planet being destructive to us. We thought even less about some outside force being destructive to our planet. We were used to hurricanes, tornadoes, floods, and earthquakes. These were inconvenient but temporary. However, the sun's nova process took the concept of natural disasters to an entirely new level. Planets and suns were big and powerful, and the nova was an extinction level event for the world we had built up over time.

Around and around I went, thinking about the deeper side of everything I had experienced so long ago. However, the thing I kept coming back to was the ET statement that they were not going to help save us. What if we had to save ourselves? ✷

16

ZigZags and Chicken Hawks

IT WAS EARLY SPRING. I HAD TO STOP EVERYTHING BECAUSE I WAS GOING TO be traveling and speaking for several weeks. I loved a chance to be behind the wheel of my car, back in what I called *windshield university* because it gave me hours of uninterrupted time to think about things deeply. I also loved meeting the people who showed up in my seminars or at my talks. They were so real and so wonderful.

As I rolled across rivers and through the mountains, I alternated between thinking about the war going on between the two factions of dinosaur elites fighting for control of the U.S., and the disruption that would come with a nova of our sun. For miles, I alternated between worry and hope, finally settling on the conclusion that both the ETs and the Robes pointed out—*we had no choice other than to develop consciousness.*

Developing consciousness was a nice thought, but then came the practical questions. What does that mean in terms of everyday living? What does that include? How do we go about doing that? How will we know if we are succeeding? In spite of all my years of teaching people about the mind and consciousness, in spite of a myriad of experiences involving out-of-body work, visits to other dimensions, and altered states of consciousness, I was not sure how to answer those questions. Personal transformation was one thing. Transformation of a civilization was something else altogether.

By the time I reached the Atlanta, Georgia area, I decided to do a little experiment with the group where I was scheduled to give a talk. I would do a ZigZag Journey. I chose seven dates to look at between the present and 2046.

In a ZigZag journey, participants do not know what dates they are looking at, and we zigzag back and forth so that they don't get caught up in a story full of personal biases that they're trying to fit together and make sense of. They don't know how far into the future I'm reaching so they can't just extrapolate from the present moment, and they only have a couple minutes to see what they see: 3-4 minutes for looking at what is going on in their personal lives, and 3-4 minutes for looking at what's going on in the greater world.

The thing that makes this kind of work so interesting is that consciousness does as directed with a minimum of the individual's usual biases, filters, and fears. I figure out how many minutes or seconds there are between the chosen dates, and then simply tell people to close their eyes and give themselves directions to move ahead from the present date X number of minutes, or move backward from the date they were just looking at X number of seconds, and they do so without being encumbered by previous ideas of what they think should be happening. Even if my number of minutes or seconds is not quite correct, I telepathically broadcast the actual date I am targeting and have learned that I can trust that this will be picked up by participants as the target date.

Participants have to write down what they see during each journey on separate pieces of paper, labeled as Journey #1, #2, etc. If there are seven dates, there will be seven pieces of paper for each participant. When we are finished I tell them the date for each journey, then ask them to put the dates in chronological order. We then go through one date at a time, each person sharing what they saw on that date, and there is often a remarkable similarity of things seen on each date.

With this particular ZigZag, we had over 50 people in the room and limited time. I had no way of recording answers from so many people, but there were two dates that stood out during the reporting. One was Nov. 30, 2021. On this date there were descriptions of "parched earth, war, food scarce." The other date was Feb. 1, 2028. On this date the descriptions included, "solar system crashing, pandemonium, chaos, fear, panic, and the word *Marrakesh.*" The woman who saw this, made it a point to talk to me the next day, saying that she had been disturbed by what she saw and heard. First, she heard the words "solar system crashing," and amid the pandemonium and chaos, she heard the word "Marrakesh." She wondered what happened in Marrakesh and if their government had collapsed or something.

I continued my trip, now grappling with the possibility that we had a date for the nova that was much closer than I wanted. For days I alternated between wrestling with how to get people more involved in shifting consciousness, and then worrying about how to survive and defend myself. Both scenarios kept coming down to a question of whether I would fight to help shift consciousness more quickly, or focus on my own life and fight to survive in the aftermath of a disaster. I didn't want to fight *against* something, yet I could not answer the question, "What would I fight *for*?" This led to the realization that I didn't want to fight at all. I turned this dilemma around and around in my mind. Then something happened that brought insights shortly after I returned home.

&

I was walking past a window that looked toward the chicken coop and noticed that I couldn't see any of my chickens in their yard. I thought that was odd, but went about my business. Later that night, I went out to close my chickens and instead of 26 chickens in the coop, there were only 25. I went back outside to see if one had gotten out of the yard and had tucked herself in the tall grasses just outside the fence. To my horror, I saw feathers scattered about and the remains of her body on the far side of the yard.

I felt so bad. The reason I hadn't seen any chickens moving around their yard earlier was because something had gotten into the yard and they were all hiding. A couple days later another one was killed. I found her, head missing, in a corner by the fence. The missing head told me that it was most likely a hawk. A few days after that, we lost a third. In frustration, I ordered some bird netting. Before it arrived, we lost a fourth chicken, and I caught the hawk in the act of eating it while the remaining chickens cowered in fear under the raised coop.

We put the netting up on a Friday evening. On Saturday morning, a baby hawk got caught in the netting and struggled to free itself until it finally died. A short time later, a huge, full-grown hawk got caught in the netting. My daughter, son-in-law, and I walked out to assess the situation. The bird tried to fly away as we approached but couldn't go anywhere. The three of us stood there gazing at the magnificent creature caught in the net. It was huge! The giant redtail gazed back at us with an intensity that was gripping. The head was much bigger than I expected, and the eyes were absolutely hypnotic. She looked at us with a power that was almost other-worldly.

After a long silence, Mike asked, "Wow, do you want me to shoot it?" Kelly and I hesitated, then Kelly replied, "Yes...no..." I knew they, too, were dealing with the same reverence for life and magnificent power of the bird just a few feet from us. I said nothing. I was wondering if there was a way to free it, but in my mind I was communicating with the hawk, telling her I hoped she had learned her lesson, that my chickens were off-limits, and that I thought we were even because I had lost four of my chickens and she had lost one baby. I asked her not to come back.

The hawk seemed to know what I was saying. She suddenly spun around, twisting in place, and took off toward the south, freeing herself in that one twisting motion. We watched her fly and join another hawk circling high above. Just then a second baby hawk flew out of the tree near the coop and joined them.

"There's a second baby!" exclaimed Kelly. I'll bet that's a mating pair. I'll bet she was looking for her baby that got caught in the net." We watched the three of them circle a bit longer before they flew off to the east. "I bet they were teaching their babies to hunt," said Mike.

"Not in my chicken yard!" I replied aloud, feeling deep relief that we had put the netting up and didn't have to shoot anything.

After this little incident, I realized several things. Yes, I would fight if I had to. My fight would begin with facing and assessing the situation. The situation just recently faced was that hawks were going to feed themselves, and my chickens were complely unprotected. I could grab a gun and start shooting, but this would only result in more grief. Better to take practical action to prevent the wholesale slaughter of chickens one by one, *and* save the hawks as well.

Other aspects of my fight would include staying abreast of changes so that I would know the status of the actual situation on the ground. This meant knowing more quickly that a baby hawk was caught in the net, in case it could be saved. The mother hawk had gotten caught in it, and so would others. The farmer side of me insisted on the importance of learning whatever skills would be needed in any fight, and of preparing for the worst while staying focused on the best that could happen because this always proved to be the most efficient use of time, money, and energy. This was a variation of the 'stitch in time saves nine' mentality.

Then there was the side of me that had been engaged in studying and researching consciousness for forty years. That side said, "In any fight, take the steps, make the changes, go out of your way, save the essential pieces, use everything you know, drop all expectations, remain alert, use common sense along with intuition and logic, be infinitely flexible, practice your power, communicate with all that exists, envision your outcomes, feel your outcomes, let go of old traumas and habits, scrub the mind clean, enter the new as if you had been waiting for it your whole life, trust the Universe to give you a boost right when you need it because it's all alive, it's all communicating, and we all know what each other needs whether that other is a bug, a bird, a planet or a person. It's time to pay attention."

ॐ

It was time to go back and take a hard look at our situation. There was more than one. Facing us was a lot of evidence pointing to a regular nova cycle of the sun. Another situation was that the U.S. was already at war. A third potential situation was that any shift of consciousness almost always resulted in a period of deep confusion and inner chaos as the entire worldview of the individual broke apart and could be followed by the breakup of marriages, finances, jobs, family relationships, religious beliefs, health, or the programming that previously steadied us. Certainly we did not want the population to be going through *that* whole process right when we needed to be paying attention to what was happening on the national and planetary scene. It took time, usually years, to get through such transitions to a more expansive worldview. Did we have enough years to make such a shift?

"Hmm, maybe the ETs were right and we're out of time. Maybe it's too late to save ourselves." But that didn't sit right with me.

Perhaps it was my stubborn Irish approach to life that kept me reaching for possibilities. Perhaps it was the part of me that loved to figure out how and why things worked, coupled with a strong dose of naivete and a touch of what my long-dead father-in-law used to call 'Yankee ingenuity," but my attitude was getting more determined by the minute. It was one of *Let's figure this out!!*

Vogt said the sun's nova and the pole shift happened together, and that the next nova cycle was due by 2046 because that was when the 12,068 years was up. The guy on MaverickStar Reloaded was predicting the pole shift in about six or seven years. That gave us between six and twenty-six years to shift the consciousness. The ZigZag journey indicated we would see it beginning by 2028.

It had taken me seventeen years to integrate the new consciousness that I stumbled into in 1979. As I reflected on my personal journey into the power of consciousness, it seemed to me that it took such a long time because I didn't know what was happening and was fearfully resisting the process with all my might. Maybe we could cut the time needed to make major changes in ourselves and our lives to half the time it took me. With a little luck, we could have just enough time to make the necessary changes in consciousness and prepare for whatever chaos might be coming with a nova. If we could do that, we could be ready for anything in only eight and a half years, which was when the "solar system crashing" had been seen in the ZigZag. ✄

17 &

The State of the Union

IN THE SPIRIT OF PREPARING FOR WHATEVER WAS COMING AT US, I WENT back to examine the information I had. My premise was, "How could I prepare correctly if I didn't know what was happening all around me in terms of people, planets, and the forces of consciousness and energy that were in motion?" I didn't want to assume that I had all the information, or that all the information I did have was correct. My thinking was that I had at least as much information as any other American citizen, and we all had to assess what was available to us and respond accordingly.

I started where I first began—with what was going on in our country. The *Robes* called this period World War III because it was a time when everyone was fighting over everything. Sadly, I had to agree.

What we had on our hands today arose from the sudden interruption of a rather nefarious plan to reorganize the entire world. This resulted in a war between two factions who each wanted to control how we will live. The control included control of the U.S. financial system and its law-making power.

The war had many fronts. The most prominent front was the fight between *nationalists* and *globalists*. The nationalists are the people of each nation. They are diverse and decentralized in terms of population and have a central government that maintains relationships with all other governments. The nationalists wanted to preserve nations and the way of life most of us were familiar with.

The globalists wanted to collapse nations into small, easily managed city-states or regions governed by one global government that controlled people, money, resources, and the balance of power on the planet. It was no longer clear if the globalists would base themselves in China in the future, but at this time, they appeared to be based in London, England, because that is where the Rothschild power base was located.

"When we speak of 'The City' we are in fact referring to a privately owned Corporation—or Sovereign State—occupying an irregular rectangle of 677 acres and located right in the heart of the 610 square mile 'Greater London' area... 'The City' is not part of England. It is not subject to the Sovereign. It is not under the rule of the British parliament. Like the Vatican in Rome, it is a separate, independent state. It is the Vatican of the commercial world...The Lord Mayor, who is elected for a one year stint, is the monarch in the City...When the Queen of England goes to visit the City she is met by the Lord Mayor at Temple Bar, the symbolic gate of the City. She bows and asks permission to enter his private, sovereign State."[96]

The Globalists had a number of names. They were loosely referred to as the *deep state* or sometimes the *shadow government*. President Eisenhower called it the *military-industrial complex*. Other people used the term *Illuminati* or the *elites*. I called them the *Cabal* because that's what they were—a secret group of corporate and political cronies working together behind our backs to overturn our government.

Regardless of what you called them, they had been working slowly and carefully for a very long time to get control of the U.S. They bought up media companies, consolidated corporate power, infiltrated intelligence agencies, and took over the presidency by electing their own members or putting puppets into office, like Bill Clinton, the Bushes, and Obama.

---

96 Griffin, Des. *Descent Into Slavery*. Emissary Publications, Clackamas, OR; 1996. P. 41–42.

A second front in the war was between *socialists* and *capitalists*. In many ways, it was a war between those who believed there could be a fair and equitable distribution of wealth, and those who felt things were good enough as is because they had benefitted from the present system. This aspect of the war often looked to me like a fight between those who wanted to be taken care of, and those who wanted self-determination.

At the top of the pyramid, there appeared to be two groups of billionaires. One group promoted socialism even though socialism required intensely detailed management. Sometimes it seemed to me that these socialist-leaning billionaires preferred a form of personal capitalism for themselves because they knew how to work the financial system, but they preferred socialism for the rest of us because they wanted to control the money, the laws, and the people at the bottom of the pyramid.

In contrast to the billionaires promoting socialism, there were other billionaires who insisted on pure capitalism for all. They, too, wanted to control money, laws, and people, however, they wanted no responsibility for whoever was at the bottom. They wanted people to sink or swim on their own decisions and efforts. They wanted people to continue working, buying corporate products, and worrying about their own bills.

Then we had the people at the bottom of the pyramid. Part of this group preferred capitalism. They did not want to be taken care of, nor did they want someone limiting them or their options. They wanted to remove the corruption that had invaded the capitalist financial system, then let the system heal and re-balance itself in a way that preserved freedom and healthy cooperation. These people were often educated enough to be able to work the system a little better than some of their fellows at the bottom.

Those at the bottom who preferred socialism wanted security, an end to poverty, and resolution of the gross financial injustice that allowed a handful of men to own 90% of the money and resources of our world, leaving the rest of us to get by on the 10% of money and resources that were left. Another problem was that some who preferred socialist policies were really choosing that path because they didn't want to worry about money or having to work too hard at something they didn't like doing. I understood this completely. After all, who wants to spend their life struggling or doing something they hate doing? They were willing to trade their power and freedom for what they believed would be a greater degree of security. I did not think this was a good or even reasonable trade. In fact, I thought it was a disastrous mistake. History shows that when we trade freedom and power for security, we end up with neither security nor freedom and power.

I wanted to see resolution of the financial gap as well, but the problem with socialism was that it required total control of every aspect of people, assets, and decision-making. We all come here to develop the self and consciousness to full potential. Handing over freedom and power goes in exactly the wrong direction. Security comes from being fully present in the moment and learning how to use your power by making decisions whose outcomes are good and teach you something. *Power is the ability to decide and do.* The development of consciousness requires presence, attention, and decision-making. If the important decisions are all made by someone else—as in a socialist situation, how can we maintain our power and relevance? The answer is...we can't. When people seek external forms of security, consciousness tends to become less attentive to reality, less creative, and there will be a degeneration of consciousness. True security comes from within.

Moving on with my analysis of where we were at, another front of the war being fought was between *Christians* and *Satanists*. On the Christian side, there was a hefty amount of infighting between Christians, Muslims, and Jews. This was greatly complicated by the fact that some of the Christians were secretly practicing Satanism. And all of them wanted to rule the world. Few people understand that power is available for those who know how to use it. Even fewer grasp the fact that power does not care whether it is used for good or for evil. Power simply *is*. We are the ones who care how it is used because we have to live with the outcomes.

Another, less obvious front being fought was the war between corporations as *persons,* and *human beings*—who had become second-rate citizens that generally lost out to the big corporations. There were also fights between Blacks and Whites, males and females, old and young, immigrants and citizens, rich and poor, Christians and Muslims, and all the other memes that kept us divided.

In surveying the situation and trying to assess things, I would sometimes I think about the New World Order and wonder why those who wanted this change didn't say so in a clear, transparent, and open manner. I remember hearing one of the Rockefellers say that he was proud to be in support of the New World Order. This was a shock to me. In his mind, he must have thought he was doing something good. If he thought it was something good, why didn't he and the others involved present it to us in a way that allowed us to see it through their eyes? Where was their excitement, their pride in something new and beautiful? Why didn't they try to sell it to us in a fair and square manner? Why did they sneak around, bribing, murdering, doing shameful things, hiding, trying to pull the wool over our eyes to make us believe we were paranoid or crazy when we said something sneaky was going on and it looked like a conspiracy? How can you set up a beautiful New World Order if you are bribing people with sex, drugs, and slush money, then murdering those who disagree? What kind of Order is *that?*

We had only heard the bad side of the NWO plan—severe reductions in population, endless wars to keep the population low, a single power to run everything using socialist or severely controlling principles, people without any say in what goes on—what population in their right mind would be interested in such an arrangement? Hadn't we risked sailing across an Atlantic Ocean in small, uncomfortable ships having no technology or weather prediction capacities in order to get away from the same problems in Europe in the Middle Ages where you had to turn your beliefs and behavior on a dime to suit whoever was currently in control? Hadn't we fought and died in a Revolutionary War in order to get away from that kind of control? Hadn't we struggled through other wars of domination to maintain freedom and the power to decide things for ourselves? Was there a good side to the NWO? If so, what was it? Why couldn't they try to sell us their ideas the way everyone else had to do?

The bottom line was that if they wanted to rule a world without nations, the globalists had to get the U.S. out of the way. Once the U.S. was collapsed and the American people with their amazing work ethic was under their control, they planned to take over the rest of the world, which would be relatively easy.

ॐ

After publishing *Trump and The Sting*, I received many letters from people who wrote to say they simply could not stand Donald Trump. To understand our situation requires some serious homework around the basics of human nature and discernment. Saying that you cannot stand Trump is akin to focusing on what color an airplane has been painted instead of whether or not it has been engineered to fly. It is the same as worrying about the uniforms an army is wearing instead of whether they know how to shoot. In both cases, the focus is on the wrong thing, which then causes disastrous decisions and bad reactions in terms of situations, needs, activities, and outcomes.

Government is not Hollywood and we cannot afford to be distracted by pretty personalities, aka identity politics. We have a situation on the planet that is ugly, hurtful, and destructive. We *need* to clean up the mess in our country or we are going to collapse. If we collapse, we will be unable to deal effectively with the sun's micro-nova process. To avoid a collapse, we must know what has been going on and how these activities have been carried out. We must work toward outcomes that are beautiful, fair, and that nurture the maturity of spirit in each individual.

It is difficult to say anything about a man as complex as Trump. In fact, I do not write about Donald Trump to make people accept him. My purpose is to expand a reader's consciousness in order to prepare for what may be coming in terms of miliary and/or civil war, and now the possibility of a natural disaster caused by the sun. However, I will say this. I have raised four children. All four of them have pretty high I.Q.s. If my memory serves me correctly, they range from 125 to 150.

It is very difficult to raise high I.Q. children because they are stunningly quick to grasp information, ideas, and intuitions about people, situations, and the world. They process information so quickly that you can hardly have a conversation with them because they are jumping ahead, interrupting with a million questions, and taking words right out of your mouth. They are frustratingly impatient because they are easily bored. They struggle when taking the path that society expects them to take—and then end up going their own way anyway.

They are laser-focused when an interesting challenge comes along, pride themselves on excellence, and tend to see the big picture as well as the details, both the usual and the unusual, in whatever type of work interests them. They are self-motivating, self-disciplined, self-organized, and self-sufficient in both their work and their personal lives.

That's all the good side. On the more difficult side, they are stubborn beyond belief because they trust their own intelligence and frequently refuse to learn from being told or by watching others. They are excruciatingly blunt, brutally honest, and the hardest things they have to deal with are taking on too much at one time, developing emotional intelligence (E.Q.), and getting a sense of timing. They take on too much because they forget there's a difference between "getting it" in terms of understanding, and "making it happen" in terms of time and labor. If trained, their emotional intelligence becomes just as powerful as their mental intelligence, but their timing in terms of sharing a moment of truth or deep feeling can be awful because they think everyone else is as quick and willing to recognize and deal with truth and feelings as they are.

Why do I share this? Because Donald Trump reminds me of my own children. He is quick to grasp and organize information, impatient with people whose thinking and conversation wanders, dawdles, or distracts from the real subject at hand. He has a broad range of experience across many disciplines, as well as life experiences that have crystallized what he wants and thinks will bring good outcomes. He is not easily fooled and therefore does not mince words. He is blunt and direct because he chooses not to waste time on stupidity or illusions, and he has taken on a *huge* challenge. His goal is to remove the corruption of the Cabal that has taken root around the entire world.

If you are someone who has been raised on a shallow diet of naiveté and cornflakes with few critical thinking skills...if you are comfortable with empty political rhetoric full of promises that never materialize...if you are someone who has been educated to think in terms of one right answer...if you are committed to religions or religious dogma above all else and believe that life here is less important than life in the hereafter because you plan on going to heaven where heavenly bliss will make up for everything you suffered while alive...if you are one of those people who are always looking for beautiful heroes that live, pure and godlike, in imaginary worlds of success without stress or the messiness of everyday reality.…if you have never really come face-to-face with your own power, then you will have difficulty with Trump.

Those who have been polarized into love or hate camps around Donald Trump are often people who think in terms of either-or. They have difficulty with the idea of *both-and*. They are uncomfortable with the true diversity that out-of-the-box thinking requires. For many polarized people, diversity is about skin color, as if skin color matters in the first place. Perhaps skin color does matter if you're buying lipstick, but true diversity means having a multi-dimensional approach to reality, something that requires a far deeper understanding of the nature of reality than most people have contemplated.

We will say more about multi-dimensional reality later, but I worry about our capacity to hold a multi-dimensional approach to anything. The American citizen has been trained to focus on movies, myths, heroes, and legends rather than reality. We have been constantly rewarded for faux psychology and belly-button gazing. We have been programmed to bow to every form of authority except our own inner authority, and we have long since forgotten how to compromise in win-win ways that honor truth while preserving the freedom and power of all concerned.

I think about the Rothschilds from time to time and cannot help but recall the vision of Mayer Amschel Bauer and his humiliation. Did it really happen? Is that what drove him to begin accumulating money and power? If it did, how do we reverse generations of frozen anger, prejudice, and persecution, especially when these feelings have spread throughout the Jewish people? How do we undo, unwind, untangle ourselves from the Rothschild system without hurting ourselves or them? How do we heal a wealthy, powerful family bent on control, steeped in fear of further humiliation, and now caught in their own web of destruction? Their situation reminded me of the chicken hawk—so intent on its mission that it failed to see the new conditions on the ground and was caught in the bird netting.

As I surveyed the state of affairs in the U.S., looking for truths while trying to rise above my own filters in the slow-to-arrive spring of 2019, it was comforting to know that what was happening here in the U.S. was also happening around the rest of the world. Italy had their Matteo Salvini, France had their Marine le Pen, England their Nigel Farage, Venezuela their Nicholas Maduro, Hungary their Viktor Orban, Austria their Sebastian Kurz, Mexico their Andres Obrador, Brazil their Jair Bolsonaro, and Indonesia their Joko Widodo. We were all fighting the same enemy—the corporate-banking Cabal that wanted to run the world their way without asking or caring what we might want.

There were a milion and one ways to connect the dots that outlined our future. If one faction of elite billionaires wanted to move the seat of power to China and collapse the U.S., and the other faction wanted that seat of power to stay in the U.S. and China-be-damned, it could all end up being a game of Collapse The Nation.

If either the U.S. or China collapsed, we would have to face massive changes in terms of governments, political activites, and the balance of power in the world. Regardless of who won, the outcome would affect everything else, especially financial aspects of life in the U.S. Were we ready for that? Given the current state of affairs, something needed to change, but the kind of change precipitated by a national collapse of either side would be like drinking from a firehose. Too much coming at us at one time.

If the Trump faction was legitimately pro-United States, and the nationalist goal succeeded in using a sting that took out the globalists as participants in a treasonous coup, we might say the nationalists won—but we would still be facing big changes. I was sure Trump was planning to implement a new energy system that was based on plasma rather than oil, as well as a new financial system based on gold because these moves would prevent a restart of Cabal power. The oil industry, along with the Federal Reserve, the World Bank, and the Bank of International Settlements were serious income streams for the Cabal, and Trump would have to end those forever in order to completely defeat them. If he succeeded he would win, but since those institutions were the base of our past greatness and success, he might be shooting himself in the foot because there could be chaos.

If the globalist goal was not to take down Trump as much as it was to destroy U.S. culture and cohesiveness, then the globalists were definitely winning—in spite of the fact that they, like the chicken hawk, were caught in the bird net right now. Chaos in the U.S. was rampant and spreading.

The catch-22 on the part of Trump nationalists was their insistence on following the rule of law and the Constitution. This was an ethical and laudable approach, but the wheels of justice might be too slow and take too long for people who had reached their limit of chaos. If the globalists continued creating mayhem, we could be facing a civil war in the U.S. because too many people could not see what was really going on or how they were being manipulated.[97] The risk was that people would end up fed up, take justice into their own hands, and throw out the entire system, baby, bathwater, and all.

If Trump succeeded in taking out the globalists, that would be great. However, if the globalists succeeded in collapsing the U.S. just as they themselves went down, then China would be the big winner. Both the U.S. and China would be free from the grip of the Cabal, but the U.S. would have collapsed, leaving only China as viable. Was this what Gordon Duff meant when he said that Trump was going to deliver the U.S. to China? I did not know.

In concluding my assessment of what was happening in our country, I decided that all we could do was work toward the world we wanted to live in. There was no other choice. To have a chance at that world, we had to take a hand in the one we were in, and that required a more awakened consciousness. &

---

97 X22 Report Spotlight. *Stolen Gold from Fort Knox Recovered – The Patriots are Now in Control.* 17 May 2019. https://www.youtube.com/watch?v=F47Ij7xDGLk. For further insight about what is going on behind the scenes, listen to this report.

18 ∂

Novas and Other Catastrophes

CONTINUING WITH A SPIRIT OF PREPAREDNESS, I TURNED TO FACE THE information about the sun and its nova process. For a brief moment, I thought about spending a little more time trying to find rebuttals that might make the information less frightening or contradict it outright, but since earlier attempts to do so only resulted in more confirmation, I decided to consider what was on the table at the moment yet leave space for new information to come in that might modify the information at hand.

The catastrophe cycle, as some called it, was becoming more widely known and was also being discussed as the theory of the solar flash. Was that how people were keeping the information at arm's length— by calling it a theory? I kept in mind the difference between a theory and a reality as I surveyed the information in front of me.

There were now a number of people on YouTube discussing catastrophic events coming at us. Many of them came across as very knowledgeable, but YouTube was notorious for spreading gossip and inflammatory stories. Should we take them seriously?

For a brief time, I wanted to discount the fact that the information about the sun's nova process had come out on YouTube instead of in a scientific paper or journal. However, as Doug Vogt pointed out, the CIA and peer-reviewed journals had carefully avoided publishing anything that got too close to the truth.

Mainstream media news was not a source for this information. In my opinion, mainstream news never said anything worth reading. Their specialty was propaganda, movie star news, and other garbage. In bygone days, the 6 o'clock news and the 11:00 p.m. news were assembled and presented to us in nice, neat perceptual packages. We had gotten used to our news being pre-digested and spoon-fed. Now, in the same way that we had begun to pump our own gas and bag our own groceries, we were learning to find, assemble, and digest our own news.

After reconsideration, I had to admit that YouTube was the only way the information could be disseminated because all other routes were closed except those considered alternative. For a day or two, I was very grateful for the Internet as a major source of information, even though I had to pick my way carefully through the jungle of reports and stories that continued to flood out every day. It was my hope that people were assembling a broad range of news and not just the news that said what they wanted to believe.

I did not want to believe we had to face the sun's nova process and in spite of the fact that earlier searches had only turned up more corroborating information, I ended up searching for anything—good or bad—that would modify the prognosis for the nova cycle. This time, I came across the work of Immanuel Velikovsky. I remembered seeing his books on a shelf in a Walden Bookstore back in the 1970s. I hadn't read any of them because I thought the subject matter was too outrageous. Now here I was, writing about the same kind of subject matter!

Velikovsky had been annihilated by the press and his scientific peers when he first published *Worlds in Collision* in 1950. Yet the only non-fiction book with more sales than *Worlds in Collision* was the Bible. I decided it was time to read it. As I read, I asked myself a question. If there were so many people out there who had read Velikovsky's book and knew of catastrophic events coming our way, why was nothing being said about periodic destructions?

I thought about the hippies of the 1960s and their free love. I had occasionally heard the comment from old hippies, "We came specifically to be here at this time!" No one ever said what they meant by the words "this time," but I always got the feeling they were referring to something that was clearly out of the ordinary, some sort of sacred duty. Was it to experience the nova? If that was the case, where were they all? Were they doing what I wanted to do—pretend I didn't know because I didn't know what to do with such information? Maybe the hippies wanted to be transported to a world like the one I had visited that was like Earth but without all the problems. Then another thought occurred to me...maybe their presence was more practical, like having enough mass consciousness on the planet to be able to totally modify swelling suns, traveling dust clouds, and rampaging oceans using consciousness that was free to communicate in deep spiritual ways that the establishment had no clue about. Those old hippies might be out of practice, but I was pretty sure they would understand what was needed if and when the need arose, because once you set spirit free, even if only momentarily, you never forget it and you're forever changed.

Spirit springs from our deepest desires, our most hidden wants, our idiosyncracies and attitudes. True spirituality is often tangled in our shadow side, the side denied because we don't know how to bring that self forward and still pay the bills, still do what family expects, still fit into the society around us. The spirit of the self is a combination of personal worldview, the personal way you go about expressing the gifts you bring to this world, and how you honor those dreams that are most important to you. As I have said many times, true spirituality is the development of the true self with all of its unique, wonderful, wacky ways.

&

I continued searching for new and hopefully more encouraging information. As I read, watched lectures, and listened, it seemed to me that a growing number of people were expressing an unconscious knowing that life on our planet and in our solar system was not nearly as stable as we had been led to believe.

Still, no one in my family was talking about this kind of thing, nor did they want to hear it when I hinted that we might have to face some serious changes. This refusal to look at the potential difficulties of being a member of our solar system was actually a good balancing influence for me. If they didn't want to hear it, maybe it was because I was way off base and needed to keep that in mind. Maybe they were saving me from myself.

If I wasn't off base, family was a good place to retreat to when I needed to get away from what I was discovering, which was that there were a number of natural cycles that could prove to be disastrous. I made a list:

- The sun's nova cycle or solar flash
- A magnetic pole shift
- The grand solar minimum (GSM) usually lasting from 30 years to several hundred years
- Global warming with an accompanying rise in sea level
- An ice-age with much colder temperatures
- The eruption of many volcanoes, including Yellowstone
- Disruption by Planet X, also known as Nibiru

The disasters produced by humans included:

- A civil war in the U.S.
- Effects and potential misuse of 5G technology
- Attacks by humans using directed energy weapons
- Attacks by humans using biological weapons

As I considered the list, it was clear to me that all of the disasters related to human activity were the result of stupidity, greed, or ignorance. We might be able to mitigate some of those, but not without serious confrontations, first with ourselves and our consciousness, and then with the powers that be.

It was also clear that all of the natural disasters on the list except for the grand solar minimum and the disruption by Planet X were related to the sun's nova cycle and were the various effects we would see at different times in that process.

The grand solar minimum was a recurring period when the sun became very quiet and there were almost no sunspots. Sunspots were the source of our warm weather. When the sun was active with a lot of sunspots creating a strong solar wind flowing around and past the Earth, the weather remained relatively stable and the planet warmed up. Sunspot activity also created a pressurized zone around the planet that prevented cosmic rays from getting into our atmosphere.

When the sun was quiet and without sunspots, its magnetic field strength fell and there was not much of a solar wind. This allowed cosmic ray particles coming through the galaxy to cascade into our atmosphere. As they did so, they disintegrated, creating the same effect as cloud-seeding. The result was the constant formation of clouds, storms, rain, hail, snow, floods in many areas, and serious cooling over all. The cooling caused the jet stream to become erratic and this caused droughts, heat waves, and a great deal of disruption in agriculture. As the Earth cooled and shrank, there were more volcanic eruptions and earthquakes.[98]

A grand solar minimum occurred about every 400 years and was often catastrophic because crops failed to mature due to cold weather, snow, and intermittent freezing all year long. Food prices rose, and in some cases, food was not available at any price. Famines spread; people went hungry. They became restless and revolutionary. This caused major changes in power structures and lifestyles. We are already a couple years into a grand solar minimum and yet few are paying attention. Even if there was no Trump and no nova, the grand solar minimum would be enough to disrupt global civilization, topple governments, and trigger mass migrations.

As for Planet X, sometimes called Nibiru or Wormwood, I had read Zecharia Sitchin years earlier and did not think much of his assertion that there was another planet coming through our solar system. I wanted to see some evidence that such a planet existed.

Over the past year or two, I came across quite a few photos from all over the world, including some from the STEREO A, STEREO B, and GOES satellites, as well as governmental camera monitoring systems in Alaska and Antarctica. They showed clearly that something was in our solar system, in fact several somethings were moving through, often covered by a chemtrailed haze.

Occasionally, I watched Steve Olson's channel, WSO, on YouTube. Olson seemed to be going through a difficult personal time, but the photos on his channel were interesting and quite unusual.

---

98 Dobler, Sacha. *The Next Grand Solar Minimum, Cosmic Rays and Earth Changes.* 14 January 2018. https://abruptearthchanges.com/2018/01/14/climate-change-grand-solar-minimum-and-cosmic-rays/

Steve was an amateur, a guy interested in astronomy and the sky. For several years he had been taking photos of his own, tracking what was going on with the sun, and sharing these along with photos that people sent him. It was obvious that strange things were going on in the skies above us. I had seen some unusual things in the skies above my own head that had no explanation except that there had to be other planetary bodies very near the Earth, and between us and the sun. This gave credence to the photos Olson and other channels were sharing, and I liked the spirit of discussion and learning that went on in the few Planet X videos I watched. No one was trying to shove answers down anyone's throat. It was mostly a collaboration of information, ideas, and refinement of those ideas based on what was actually being observed.

In my view, the biggest threat of a real Planet X was that it was said to be seven to ten times larger than the Earth. If that was the case, then its magnetic fields would be much bigger and stronger than the magnetic fields of the Earth. Since it was coming up from below the Earth, its north magnetic pole could lock on to our south magnetic pole. As it then continued to move up and beyond us, it could drag our south pole up with it, tipping us over and causing serious earthquakes and damage along all coastlines. Since more than 53% of the global population lives on the coasts[99] along with many large corporations and warehouses filled with goods and products that have been shipped or are waiting to be shipped, half our world could be destroyed by a planet that was said to come wandering through our solar system every 3,600 years. I wanted to disbelieve the whole Planet X story just like I wanted to disbelieve the story of the sun's nova, but now there was evidence. Even if half the photos on the Internet were faked and photoshopped, there were still a lot that needed to be explained and taken into account. Even if 99 out of 100 photos were fake, how would we explain the one that wasn't a fake?

I looked again at the cycles of natural disasters on my list. All were due or overdue, and all had effects that were pretty powerful. It would

---

99 *How many people live by a coast?* Yahoo Answers. https://answers.yahoo. com/question/index?qid=20081210175407AA71UNO

not be easy for a technological civilization like ours to cope with such effects. Yet regarding the sun's nova, I began to see that some of the factors mentioned earlier might help to lessen the impacts on us, improving our chances of survival.

One factor mentioned by a number of researchers was that as we neared the point of the micro-nova, the sun would enlarge. This would be a physical sign that the nova was close and this would give us time to make final preparations, or go to the destination we wanted to be at, increasing the odds for survival.

Another factor was that if the magnetic field around the Earth dropped off, our rate of rotation would slow down. Doug Vogt pointed out that as this occurred, we might experience longer days of 25- to 27-hour days. I chuckled at the idea I might finally have more time to get things done each day! However, the real benefit would be that any slowdown in our rotation would mean that the oceans were also slowing, which would give us a better chance of keeping the oceans in their basins instead of rolling across the entire continent if and when the rotation stopped altogether.

For many years, we all listened to reports of melting ice at the north and south poles. These reports were used to frighten us and make us feel guilty that such a thing was happening, but maybe this melting was one of the ways that Mother Nature tried to reduce the trauma to the Earth before a micro-nova occurred. If a micro-nova situation caused a gradual drop in magnetic field strength around the earth...and this drop caused a slowing in the rotation of the planet...and a slowing of the planet's rotation caused any loads of heavy ice at the north and south poles to tip over until the ice and the poles were at the equator or whatever point would produce a new balance between the two ice loads.. then the fact that some ice had melted might result in less tendency to roll over, therefore less damage and less trauma for all.

Stories of melting ice were always presented as a climate disaster that was the result of increasing carbon dioxide (CO_2), but I thought this was bunk. Since I knew plants and trees grew much better in an atmosphere that is rich in CO_2, my personal attitude was that, given the amount of destruction going on in the natural world, the extra carbon dioxide was a boon to our green friends struggling to survive.

Those pushing the need to reduce carbon dioxide in order to stop the melting ice that was said to be causing sea level rise were really just pushing a carbon tax that they insisted was needed to fine corporations that were producing CO_2. I couldn't see what benefit this would have for the world. They only benefit was to politicians' bank accounts.

From my perspective, a carbon tax was a secret signal that a new form of energy had been developed and was going to be introduced. It signaled that elite corporations pulling the strings of government had finished mapping out a new form of energy and were now ready to play games in the energy sector. The carbon tax was a way to start pressuring and penalizing those in the old businesses that produced energy from fossil fuels. It was a way to squeeze a little more money out of what would soon be a dying business, perhaps killing it off completely. It was also a way of challenging various energy players to see who would recognize the hidden game and get on board as an early adopter, take out the necessary loans to complete the development of infrastructure, and carry all the risk of such a venture. It was a way to force change without spending a dime, yet having complete control over the final energy system and its resources because it would be deemed a "public utility."

It reminded me of what happened with alcohol in the early part of the 20th century. Thomas Edison invented an internal combusion engine that ran on alcohol and a battery that ran for 100 years on alcohol,[100] but the big bankers wanted cars to run on gasoline because the regular purchases of gas would make them more money. They got Congress to outlaw alcohol in all forms and the result was Prohibition. By the time Prohibition was repealed, the development of cars based on gasoline was far enough along that nobody was interested in using alcohol.

Going back to look at factors that might help mitigate the nova catastrophe, I considered the fact that Doug Vogt and other scientists had talked about the evaporation of hundreds and possibly more than a thousand feet of water off the surface of the oceans. This would reduce the amount of water that could go speeding across the continents in a huge

100 Riger, BZ AM. *Trump the greatest actor of all time - A hypothesis.* I UV Blog, 21 April 2019. https://i-uv.com/trump-the-greatest-actor-of-all-time-a-hypothesis/

wave. It might give us another little edge in favor of survival, however, all that water would then be up in the atmosphere and come pouring down on us in the form of rain and snow.

I thought about the story of Noah, the flood, and the report of forty days of rain. Early in my life, I thought it was an inspiring story. As I became more educated, I scoffed at notions of such a flood. Now it looked like a deluge was part of the aftermath of the sun's nova. A thousand feet of water was a lot of rain, and 19,000 feet of snow would be worse, especially in a location that didn't melt quickly and easily. Four hundred or eight hundred or 1,200 feet of water coming down as rain was almost unimaginable. I freaked out when we got 8 inches of rain during a particularly bad storm 20 years ago.

Higher ground might be the solution for that part of the challenge, but it would have to be a lot higher. How many people would a mountain hold? Certainly not 7 billion of us! And what if the land the mountain was sitting on suddenly sunk and the mountain ended up below the sea? What if lowlands were pushed up high and we ended up on a new version of Mount Everest without a way to get down safely? I thought about Lake Titicaca in South America. It had once been at sea level and in one of the cataclysms it was moved up 12,000 feet above sea level. Obviously land masses became very fluid during the nova cycle. Velikovsky had agreed.

Maybe we could use the time we had left to create shelters and bunkers to ride out the worst of the catastrophe, but how would we know where to build these?

The information coming from MaverickStar Reloaded was that both the north and south magnetic poles had recently split into two poles each. There was a magnetic north pole in Canada, and another one in Siberia. There was a magnetic south pole off the northeast corner of Australia, and another one off the west coast of Peru. We had no way of knowing if the poles would move to other locations during the shift, or what these locations would be. What if we built shelters that ended up at one of the poles and found ourselves trapped there? Even if groups of people found shelter and places to survive, would they be able to live together and get along for a year or more if they were crowded into bunkers, caves, or underground tunnels? A lot of people couldn't even drive down the same street with others and not end up in a rage.

If the sun's nova could be predicted, could we move people over to one side of the Earth so they wouldn't be fried by the heat? That would save them from the heat, but it would subject them to the ungodly frigid temperatures that occurred when the earth's atmosphere expanded to fill in the atmosphere that had been blown away by the dust cloud. Maybe we could do like the elites had done and dig big underground tunnels and cities, but what would keep them from leaking once the rain started? Was there time for that, or would the time be better spent developing consciousness?

&

While assessment of the nova information was going on, I remembered a dream I had in April of 2000. In the dream, I was standing at the back door of the building talking with Jim on a beautiful summer morning when I saw a trickle of water moving across the ground. Suddenly a huge wall of water at least 35 feet high, filled with mud, trees, parts of houses, animals, chicken coops, farm equipment and things from people's lives came over the northwest hill, sweeping across the landscape toward us. Instantly, I turned and ran down the main hallway thinking I needed to get to the fourth floor, but the wall of water hit the building before I got even half way down the hall. I felt the building shudder, heard lumber cracking and windows breaking, and I knew that this was it, the end, my life was over. I woke in terror, coming back to the body so quickly that I felt like my body was a liquid for a few minutes and nothing worked right until all the bits and pieces of liquid were back in place and solid again.

I never forgot that dream. I could not get over the wall of water that came racing toward us out of the northwest. Now I thought about the dream and wondered if it had been a warning of what was to come.

Until that moment, when I thought about the nova cycle, I worried about the problem of oceans splashing onto the land, but what if it was water from Lake Michigan? I was about 35 miles from the Lake Michigan coast and fairly sure that any water from the lake would not be able to reach me, however, I could not stop worrying about this. Finally, I got out a pencil and paper and sat at my computer to do a little research and figuring.

There were six quadrillion gallons of water in Lake Michigan! The lower peninsula of Michigan was about 400 miles from south to north. I was about 35 miles from the lake. There were 5,280 feet in one mile.

I started by multiplying 35 miles x 5,280 feet per mile and got 184,800 feet from my house to the coastline. I then multiplied 400 miles x 5,280 feet per mile to get a total of 2,112,000 feet for the north-to-south length of the west Michigan coast. Then I multiplied these two numbers to get the number of square feet starting at the water's edge and moving inland 35 miles from top to bottom of lower Michigan and got 184,800 ft. x 2,112,000 ft. = 390,297,600,000 sq. ft.

If we imagined that our wall of water was 1 foot deep, we could convert our 390,297,600,000 square feet to cubic feet. One cubic foot of water was equal to about 7.5 gallons. Therefore, a one foot deep wall of water reaching from the coast to at least 35 miles inland would use up 390,297,600,000 cu.ft. x 7.5 gal. = 2,927,232,000,000 gallons of water, which, in math-speak, was 2.9 trillion gallons. If we made the wall of water 10 feet high, we would use 29,272,320,000,000 gallons of water or 29.2 trillion gallons. A 20-ft. wall of water would use 58,544,640,000,000 gallons or 58.5 trillion gallons, and we were still only in the trillions of gallons used. Doubling the height to 40 feet, would finally get us to the point of using one quadrillion gallons, but that did not even begin to tap the amount of water in the lake. With six quadrillion gallons moving over us, the wall of water would be six times higher—240 ft. high!

I was notorious for bad arithmetic when it came to spatial figuring, so I hoped maybe I had something figured wrong, but it looked to me that Lake Michigan was going to be just as much a problem as the oceans if the planet stopped rotating and the water kept going.

Once again, it was looking like the only option we had was to develop consciousness. I had a fair amount of experience talking to the wind, the rain, the sun, and other forms of intelligence in Mother Nature. So did other people! Sometimes groups of people would get together and ask a hurricane to change course—and it would! Could we make a concerted effort to develop our relationships with these other forms of consciousness who shared the reality with us and in doing so, lessen the effects of the nova cycle?

I had created a series of nine meditations to heal the Pacific Ocean after the Fukushima nuclear disaster and people found them to be educational, inspiring, and helpful. After they were up on the website, I began to hear conflicting reports about Fukushima. Some said the radiation was destroying everything, while others said the radiation had mysteriously disappeared. At first, I didn't pay much attention to either side in this conflict, but later I wondered if the conflicting reports were coming from two different earths or maybe two different reality systems, one of them started by those of us who had spent time envisioning a healed Fukushima and Pacific Ocean and who loved Packy—my name for the Pacific.

There didn't seem to be any quick and easy answers. Frequently I would get upset about the situation we were in. How did we get here? Where was our leadership? Where was the common sense that would have us assess the situation and challenges, invite the population to work together to come up with ideas, solutions, strategies, and task lists? Why didn't they bring the best available resources to bear on those challenges? Why hadn't we developed all our amazing technology into useful, peaceful applications?

Was it because we didn't have leaders? In fact, it looked like all we had were strongmen. Strongmen were not interested in solutions that included all of us. They were power-hungry and too often willing to hurt others. I knew I was complaining, but I was tired of strongmen. I wanted to hear something encouraging, see something wonderful that showed the way into a bright and promising future. All I could think was that we were at the mercy of strongmen who had seized everything we needed to survive. But were we?

❧

19

Out of Time?

NATIONS MAY NOT BE A FOREVER THING, BUT THEY TEACH A SET OF POWERFUL organizing principles that fill a critically needed stage in the evolution of people and planets. If a nation collapses, it is important to hang onto the principles learned, principles like how to live together peacefully; organize a neighborhood; supply food, heat and electricity; take care of sewage; make rules that guide everyone without oppression; share art and music; handle trade and education; or decide what to do about rogue members. Whatever the organizational form, be it a nation or a village, when it breaks down or becomes disorganized, these principles of civilization are often lost. People go back to primitive living and start again.

Millions of people have not yet awakened to the fact that we have been mucking around in the bottom of a very deep pit and are now trying to climb out of it. Even though we have worked harder and harder over the past fifty years, the number of impoverished and homeless people has grown exponentially. We are bankrupt, facing China from a one-down position, trying to buy time to position ourselves more favorably, and realizing we wasted our social capital in every country we worked in because we thought we would always be on top in terms of power.[101]

---

101 X22 Report Spotlight. *Stolen Gold from Fort Knox Recovered–The Patriots are Now in Control.* 17 May 2019. https://www.youtube.com/watch?v=F47Ij7x-DGLk.

When listening to the media, whether mainstream or alternative, for even a few minutes, you hear the phrase over and over about "trying to get rid of Trump…hating Trump…taking down Trump…blocking Trump…" Don't be fooled.

The criminal Democrats, Republicans, Left, Right, and media are NOT trying to get rid of Trump, they are working to save their own asses, trying to avoid prosecution for the horrendous crimes committed, trying to avoid going to jail. It's not really about Trump at all, it's about *them and their efforts to avoid discovery and prosecution.* Of course, it's too late for that. Trump and team are uncovering their deeds, shining some light on how badly they have used power and money. Even though many are being revealed as criminals, they are still trying to accomplish their goal of taking down the United States. If they can keep us divided, they are hoping we will do the job of taking down the U.S. for them.

I love Donald Trump's invitation to *Make America Great Again*, but—we can't go back. We must go forward. Our government has been so corrupt for so long that a lot of young people and even those in their 50s and 60s think this *is* forward. They don't see that we are back to the indentured status of people in Rome who sold themselves as slaves or servants when they needed money or favors. They think the size of government is normal. The functions that I think of as fawning interference and government over-reach, they think are signs that government cares. Most of the processes that I see as corrupt, they see as ordinary. There are plenty of people who don't care about normal or ordinary, they just care about being comfortable.

Changes are difficult for those who are comfortable and want to stay that way. People howl when the economy crashes. They become activists when something changes in the education system or the price of gas goes up. They end up fighting a single change, not realizing that they are fighting a paradigm change. If anything in the base paradigm changes, everything else is going to change as well. They might better spend their time understanding the implications of the change and making intelligent preparations for it. If our form of government changed, if the size of government changed, if the functions of government changed, those who have been comfortable would be seriously uncomfortable.

The Trump team made it clear from the start that they were going to drain the swamp, translated as "take out those involved in the corruption," which is deeper, more evil, and more widespread than many have suspected. The Trump team has committed themselves to doing this clean-up quietly and with minimal disturbance for the American people. This is good…but only to a point.

It bears repeating; I'm concerned that not enough people see what is really going on. If the Trump team carries out their sting *too* quietly, people will not see beyond the narrative created by the mainstream press. They will not understand that something good is happening in the background because they are unaware of the massive corruption and fraud that has overtaken our political, financial, pharmaceutical, religious, legal, and other systems.

Completely indoctrinated to chase after Hollywood-style heroes, many complain about Trump's language or attitude, believing they can find a handsome, god-like leader without flaws. This is akin to needing rescue from a flood then refusing to get on board the boat that comes to rescue you because the captain isn't Keanu Reeves or Tom Cruise. We must begin to see how we are being manipulated to stay divided and at each other's throats. Otherwise we will tear our country apart.

We are at war. I tried to deny it, but I have been watching this war slowly take shape since the visits from the Robes many years ago. Even with their advance notice of what we were moving toward, I ignored the situation for years and kept telling myself it would all be okay. So far, the war has been relatively hidden. As far as most people are concerned, it has been a war of words, policies, and court appointments. It is not a hot or kinetic war in the ways that WWI and WWII were, but it's still war.

The battles are taking place between Donald Trump and the Cabal of billionaires who run our lives through their banks and corporations. There are battles taking place in courtrooms where lawyers use the rule of law to try to re-establish order and compliance with our Constitution. There are battles between mainstream media outlets that pump out propaganda, and a gaggle of alternative news channels that struggle to keep the real news flowing so we know what is really going on. There are battles in banking circles to maintain control of the thousands of tons of hidden gold, the Black Eagle Trust, and the secret computer codes that keep track of this wealth.[102] There are hidden raids conducted by our military to disrupt the income streams from drugs and human trafficking that keep the Cabal afloat. There are battles on our border to prevent the U.S. from being overrun by immigrants who have a host of agendas, few of them good or noble. There are battles between the Christians trying to stop pedophilia, child sex trafficking, and human sacrifice, and the Satanists who practice these things because they believe it brings them power. If the Robes are right and we do not develop ourselves, there will be a civil war that will result in the break-up of the U.S. into several regions.

Courtesy of the Robes, I saw and walked in the world of the future. A lot of people were gone. This bothered me at the time, and I asked what happened to everyone. They said only that "most people left in the first 25 years of the new millenia,' and here we are. I didn't connect the tiny population to idea that only a few developed consciousness enough to survive. It didn't dawn on me that there was a reason that the first thing they showed me was the Earth rolling and bobbing around in space. It didn't dawn on me that we would not survive to create the future they showed me without a more developed consciousness. I thought the Robes wanted us to develop consciousness because it was the nice thing to do. I thought it was because they didn't want the U.S. to to break up or suffer another civil war.

Now, forty years later, I'm seeing that except for our technology and our anger, we didn't develop anything. If we had matured a little sooner and recognized what was really going on, we might have been able to come together as a country and prepare for whatever the sun might send our way. Now, both challenges are in our face. Are we are out of time? We might be able to salvage the country enough to come together and do what we can to prepare for Earth changes, but it would take a Herculean effort to pull it off. ❧

---

102 If you would like to get an idea of the scope of the corruption, read *Financial Tyranny* by David Wilcock, or *Gold Warriors* by Sterling and Peggy Seagrave, or *The Creature from Jekyll Island* by G. Edward Griffin.

20 &

Reality is a Joint Venture

WHO ARE WE? HOW DO WE WANT TO LIVE? THIS IS *OUR* REALITY SYSTEM. Each of us contributes to it with every thought, word, and deed. We all agree on the two basics—that we will have a reality based on the concept of an individual existence, and the principle of non-interference. That's it. The rest is a conglomeration of individual contributions that we tolerate, celebrate, duplicate, erase, or try to ignore. Some of it works smoothly, some not, but it's all our creation.

How does one coax an entire culture to grow up and recognize that Santa Claus does not exist and neither do the many related religious fairytales? These are like childhood stories written to entertain and teach the immature mind. The goal is for each person to grow to full spiritual maturity. When we don't mature, we end up telling these fairytales again and again to cover up a lost understanding of our past and the potential hidden in our consciousness. If we are going to navigate this passage in our world, we must mature enough to understand the true nature of reality.

The nature of reality is simple. Everything that exists is made of space, and space is alive and aware. I think this is why people are afraid to be alone. It's because something in them knows they are not alone—ever! They sense there is something out there, something enormous, but they can't see or hear it, which scares them. What they're sensing is the vast awareness of space that they are made of and that surrounds, enfolds, and connects them to every living thing that exists—*and it's all alive!* The movement of space creates waves, also known as frequencies, and it is the ability of frequencies to produce particles that self-organize, which results in an individual. You and I are a bunch of frequencies and fields.

Frequencies and fields are the basis of what science calls *energy*, and since frequencies *are* space in motion, they inherit the awareness of space and turn it into consciousness. Since everything in existence is made from the ocean of space with its waves or frequencies, that means everything in existence is aware and conscious. Since everything in existence is aware and conscious, that means you can communicate with everything whether it is a person, a tree, a bird, an ocean, or a planet.

&

When I was doing research for *Consciousness and Energy, Volume 3*, I read something that affected me deeply, I can't remember where I read it, but the remark, or perhaps it was a protest, came from the Pagans after the Catholic Church forbade them, under pain of death, to look at the stars or to practice the old religion, known as the Goddess religion. This religion included many rituals that were designed to communicate with Nature in an effort to manage the world and make things go smoothly. The protest went something like, "...but the system won't work without our input!" They were talking about the system of Mother Nature needing input from her resident humans. Ancient peoples knew that this reality system needed input from all participants.

Let me share an experience from my own life. I have talked about this in some of my talks or interviews, but it bears repeating here because it illustrates an important point.

I had a couple of workmen here to put up some siding and roofing over the main kitchen at the back of the building. They were working outside, and I was working in my office. There are no windows in my office, and with two floors above me, there was no way to see or hear that the weather changed.

After a couple hours, the men came to my office door and said that they were done for the day because it was raining. "You might have to put some buckets out," they said. "We tried to cover it the best we could, but it's coming down pretty hard..."

I didn't even give them a chance to finish. I bolted from the office and went racing to the back kitchen where I ran out on the porch, raised my hands to the sky, and shouted, "Sto-o-o-op!" with great passion. The rain stopped immediately.

I stood there for a minute, hands still raised, then as if to reinforce what I needed from the rain, I said, "And don't start again until these guys are done!"

The two men were standing in the doorway staring at me with mouths agape. I looked at them and said a single word in an urgent voice, "Hurry!!!" They set to work immediately and I went back to work in my office. It wasn't until later that evening that I had time to reflect on what happened and how instantly the rain stopped. Belatedly, I was feeling a little surprised.

Not long after that, I was talking with one of the elves on my farm with whom I've had a long relationship. I asked Alvey why the elements responded to me, and yet other people complained that nothing happened when they tried such things.

"Because you have a relationship!" Alvey said. "Consider what would happen if you were sitting in your living room and a stranger ran in off the street and demanded you give him a hundred dollars. Your response would be to tell him to get out, and you would probably call the police. Why? Because you don't know him, and you don't have a relationship with him. If that was your child or a friend, your response would be different."

This was the first time I recognized the value of all those times I said "Good morning!" to the birds as I walked out to feed chickens or cows. It was the first time I realized the importance of just touching base with the sun, blowing a kiss to the wind, saying hello to the trees, going to visit them or touching them as I walked by, and other little things that showed I recognized them as individuals in my world.

Transforming consciousness is not something that is done in a day. It takes time, practice, and integration. It takes common sense, physical effort, and practical experimentation. Above all, it takes patience, humility, and a spirit of adventure anchored in love. Millions of people have been programmed to believe that transformation is something magical that mysteriously happens to you, and in some ways it is. But there are a lot of tears and a lot of work to get to that place of power. Even when you get there, it is not something you own.

You can make a decision at any moment to change consciousness, but then you have to do the work required. Until you *feel* different inside, nothing has changed. Feeling is a characteristic of frequency, and you are a collection of frequencies. Together, these frequencies create a physical vehicle in the center of a large sphere where the frequencies are the most densely packed. Picture yourself as a sphere of frequencies that are cohesive and working together as one identity—*you*.

Everything in our reality is formed by frequencies and their accompanying electromagnetic (EM) fields and particles. We refer to frequencies as *energy*. Every frequency carries its own bit of awareness, consciousness, and intelligence. Frequencies don't just carry consciousness, they *are* consciousness. When we talk about a change in consciousness, we are really talking about a change in frequencies, their associated E-M fields, and the particles that the frequencies produce. Since everything within our reality is held in place by the interaction of these frequencies and fields, changing consciousness changes these interactions. Sometimes the shifting interactions become visible, but even when they are not visible, they can be felt because changes in frequency result in changes in feeling. *Feeling is primary*. Some people have to get hit with a telephone pole before they feel anything. If you can't feel the change you want to make, then you are fooling yourself about anything having changed. The ability to notice and track subtle changes in frequency is a skill that comes from a form of intelligence known as *intrapersonal intelligence*.[103]

---

103 Gardner, Howard. *Frames of Mind; The Theory of Multiple Intelligences.* Basic Books, Philadelphia, PA. 1983.

You may talk about *higher* consciousness, but what you are really talking about is an *expansion* of your core frequencies. When core frequencies shift or expand, it creates changes in perception and the entire energy body. This changes how you feel, see, and hear, as well as how you think and act, because seeing, hearing, feeling, and action are all expressions of frequency. Once this expansion occurs, you will see, hear, and feel much more—both good and bad—which often brings tears. You begin communicating with other spheres of energy (people, plants, animals, and the elements) much more clearly. You can also begin communicating with other dimensions as well (ETs, other timelines, and foreign worlds).

The real change in consciousness—the move into your power—comes when you begin to examine and evaluate the meanings you assign to words and other events. (Yes, a word is an event.) This is the work referred to above. Most of our meanings have been programmed into us between ages of 2 and 7 years. If you hear a certain tone of voice, you have learned to cringe in fear. If someone spits at you, you have been programmed to feel insulted and get angry. If someone smiles at you, you warm up to them. But what if tone of voice no longer controlled you? What if spitting meant something else? What if the smile was entrapment?

A core change in consciousness is, 1) A change in frequency, 2) A change in meaning, and 3) Involves an expansion that expands the dense frequencies in the core self without losing communication between and among those frequencies. In other words, your density changes. Once this expansion happens, it allows other frequencies carrying new information to move through you, sharing their information as they pass, which is why there are moments of insight, moments of precognition, clairvoyance, and gut knowing.

&

If we were going to create a To-Do list for developing consciousness, we could start with the following:

1. Begin by making a conscious decision to expand consciousness and step into your power. Write this intention down or create a symbol that will represent this decision and put it where you will see it and be reminded of your goal each day.

2. Start looking at your environment and seeing who is around you—really seeing as if for the first time. Practice the discipline of observing instead of reacting. A good way to practice this is to pretend you are a ghost quietly watching without interfering. This leads to the development of the Observer Self and a feeling of detachment while you see everything going on around you.

3. Practice suspending judgment one day, then switch to making instant intuitive judgments the next day. Alternate back and forth, noticing when the suspension is useful, and when the intuitive judgment is correct. The goal is an increase in fluidity, and is related to #2 above, developing your ability to detach yourself from programmed responses to life.

4. Start communicating with Mother Nature, as well as the things you have brought into your life such as your car, your dishes, a favorite tool or piece of equipment, your flower garden, the tree in the yard, the clerk at the grocery store, or the pot of soup you are making. The idea is to develop gratitude and appreciation for all forms of life and the goal is to begin establishing relationships based on recognition of others' presence and their role in your reality.

5. Learn to listen and respond at the whole-body-feeling level to what you hear. This includes listening to people, animals, equipment, insects, the wind, the highway, the trees, etc. Skip the thinking and just practice feeling your response to what you hear through your entire body.

6. Do not try to get rid of old angers or fears. Initially, these are useful forms of powerful emotion to be hauled out of emotional closets when needed and paired with intent in order to make something happen. You can identify the angers or fears, and practice moving into the intensity of the feeling, but then move out of it without changing it. I know this flies in the face of all popular psychology, but try not to worry about that right now. Your goal is to get to the point that you are only roused to intensity by those things that are yours to respond to, yours to act on, change, or heal. An important

point here is that a powerful healer doesn't heal everyone. Some people are not his to heal. He can only heal those who spark an intense response within him. Ditto for any change agent. Some things are not yours to deal with. You will know what is yours to deal with because it will spark an intense and instant reaction in you, and a desire to step up and do something. When this happens, energy and power are on your side. Go with it. Eventually the full development of spirituality heals all anger and fear, leaving you in a place of peace until something that is yours to deal with arises.

7. Understand that quiet, prayerful, milk-toast requests often go nowhere. To get a response from the Universe, you have to have a clear intent AND be able to merge powerful feeling with that intent. This takes a bit of practice, but at the moment of crisis, you must not panic, or throw your hands in the air and give up. You must stand your ground, know what you want (intent) and be able to merge that knowing with strong feeling (emotional power) in a commanding way. People often perceive anger or challenge as something bad. They allow themselves to drop into victim mode. This is a total waste of power. Get a grip on your emotions and marry that power to something you want to see happen in this world. See #6.

8. In addition to using angers and fears (which weaken the more they are used consciously) there are many ways to stir up the energy needed to drive intent: sexual activity, dance, chant, rituals, breathwork, fasting, carrying out symbolic behaviors, visiting or talking with someone who challenges you or stimulates you intellectually, and learning when to censor yourself and when to go with the energy, riding it to its destination. Explore some of these ways of generating strong energy and learn what you are good at.

9. Learn to recognize the signs that the energy around you has changed or is changing. Reality wraps around us like a glove around a hand. If we shake a hand, reality shakes back. If we use our hands to form a cup, reality fills it. The point is that reality is very dynamic and much more fluid than you think. When any

of the frequencies within a space are changed, you may see the change in small flashes of light out of the corner of your eye, or a change in light levels in the room. When we move past the rigid thinking that we are only able to communicate with other people, and start communicating with everything that exists, we find that it's *all* alive, it's all listening, it's all responding. A wall doesn't have a mouth, so don't expect it to speak words to you. But it can expand, pop, crackle, snap, or bend because it has consciousness and a bit of fluidity, just like you and I. Plants communicate by releasing smells, and sometimes they wave. Animals, birds, and bugs are afraid of us, and rightly so, because we are often callous and indifferent to them and what is going on with them. However, they are delighted when we bother to talk with them. Clouds will part briefly when you want to see the sun. The wind will slow down or speed up if you ask it to. The rain will stop or start in response to your request, bacteria will leave an area of the body where they aren't wanted, and things will appear and disappear depending on your mood, your intensity, and your ability to shift the field of frequencies surrounding you. Picture yourself as just one set of frequencies within an entire ocean of frequencies that make up your local reality. Everything is frequency, and frequencies maintain specific relationships to one another. You have seen this in the way two bar magnets will move together or apart depending on how their frequencies and fields are oriented. Consider yourself to be a living bar magnet who has just never oriented yourself to notice your impact on things and never bothered to learn how to manage that impact.

10. Experiment with fasting and note how consciousness changes when you are not loaded down with food. Learning how to breathe correctly greatly eases hunger. Directing your breath right into the center of an area of great discomfort, whether that is the stomach or some other location in the body, will relieve that discomfort immediately or at least push it to the background.

11. Learn to grow food, to preserve food, or to sew, fix small equipment, or anything you think would be a useful skill. Start

small and don't overwhelm yourself. Not only are these key skills for maintaining yourself, they are useful and powerful forms of meditation.

12. Practice remembering your dreams and becoming lucid. Just sit on the edge of the bed for a few minutes every night and remind yourself that you will remember your dreams, or that you will become lucid within a dream. When you are lucid, you are in the very special position of being able to move energy and decide what the movement of that energy will accomplish in the physical world because the result will transfer. If you do become lucid in a dream, know what you want to accomplish. Take the time to think about what you want to see or make happen before going to sleep. Hold that intent until the moment comes that you can apply it. If the moment comes when you are in a lucid dream, you will discover that, quite often, very little energy is needed to bring about the desired outcome. All you need is the intent of knowing what you want, and an accompanying deliberate movement or action within the dream reality that represents the act of accomplishing what you want to happen in the physical reality.

13. Start up a conversation with an animal or an insect. It can be verbal or telepathic. Note what happens. The reaction of most people before beginning this is usually doubt about whether anything will happen. Do not look for anything spectacular or outlandish to occur, just have a simple conversation. When a response comes into your mind from the animal, don't discount it. You are practicing telepathy. Honor what comes to you and respond appropriately. Sometimes the animal or bug will hear you and not respond. They are just like people and have their crabby or irritable days. But sometimes they truly respond with both telepathic communications and behavior. Try not to act shocked. Monitor your breathing and follow the direction the conversation is going. Sometimes your reaction to a real conversation and behavior change on the part of an animal or insect is delayed shock. This is often followed by low-level fright. Why? Because we are afraid of power. Most people didn't think it would work

(as if it were a trick of some sort). They didn't think that was how reality worked, and no one ever told them they could talk with Nature and Nature would talk back! The common reaction is surprise and then a bit of fear. Do not be afraid of your own power. This kind of communication used to be common.

14. Choose an element in Nature to work with. For example, decide you are going to learn to communicate with the sun, the wind, the ocean, the Earth, or fire. Introduce yourself to that element and state your reason for wanting to get to know it. Be honest and straightforward. You might try starting up a relationship with one element but feel you're not getting anywhere. In that case, switch. When you find an element that responds to you, make the effort to have regular conversations with it. Keep it simple at the start. Note how the relationship evolves. Keep it going. Do not ask for frivolous favors or things you don't really need. You do not develop consciousness so you can show off. You develop it so you can use it when you truly need it.

15. Experiment with telepathic communication by telepathically asking someone for a favor, to be understood, or forgiven, perhaps to give someone permission to do what they want or need to do. This can be done by talking to the other-than-conscious side of them to let them know what you would like to have happen. We are all communicating telepathically all the time. We are listening to one another at deep levels because we care. Use a consistent form of telepathic address when you contact someone. 1) Say hello and state your name, 2) Say, "I would really appreciate it if you would ...." (state your wish), 3) Communicate your gratitude, "Thank you so much, I truly appreciate it..." 4) Then formally close the communication by saying, "I am closing now."

16. Experiment with healing yourself and others using consciousness, which is frequency. In addition to using hands-on healing such as massage, reiki, or other techniques, you can heal people, animals, yourself, or a difficult situation by sending someone energy. In directing energy to others, you must hold the clear intent of what you want in the forefront of consciousness, envision the person

or situation, and then visualize the change—all at the same time. If you are truly moving energy to that individual, you will see a change in how they appear in your envisioning of them, or you will hear a loud pop, crack, or sizzle as the energy moves. One of the workmen who does repairs for me had liver cancer. I really liked him and his work, and I didn't want to lose him, so I took on the task of regularly sending energy to "Tom Smithson's Liver" (not his real name). I would picture his liver and visualize beautiful golden-white energy with pink edges filling it. The liver always appeared as kind of dried out and shrunken until one day, it spontaneously plumped up, became a rich, dark-crimson color, and looked amazingly healthy. Two weeks later I happened to ask him how he was doing with his chemo and he said, "I just got the latest report back and the size of the tumor is half of what it was before." I continue to work on him. When you have had an effect on someone, you may also hear a sound when your efforts have that effect. The sound comes from the movement, reorganization, or response of the frequencies that comprise the local reality around you and the target individual. It is the confirmation that you have changed something.

17. We are a civilization that is faced with the choice of evolving to a new level of consciousness or disintegrating into chaos. Practice opening your heart to someone or something. Do things that awaken your gratitude for life. Some people meditate. Some watch humorous YouTube videos of animals. Some garden, others cook. The best way to generate gratitude is to do something you love doing. Let yourself love...and let that love change you.

As we consider ways to develop consciousness, we have to ask ourselves, "What are we going to do with it once it's developed?" Given our current set of oncoming possibilities, let's look once again at the concept of superposition, which would say that the Earth exists in every possible state until the moment you try to locate or measure it. The moment you try to identify some aspect of it, the whole thing crystalizes into what you are trying to measure. In other words, it becomes what you expect.

I have been to an Earth that was extremely beautiful, clean, and where everything and everyone was exquisitely conscious, thus, I know from personal experience that at least one other Earth exists. I did not create it, but someone must have. That new Earth had a different kind of social organization that did not involve the kind of politics or finance that we have here. The rules of communication were based on telepathy, and the rules of relationship were based on total cooperation and unconditional love. The people living there said I would have to give up all my ideas about how a reality should operate, but nothing I saw or experienced was disagreeable.

The question is, could we develop consciousness enough to go there? How would we get there? I have been to that Earth three times by invitation and once on my own by accident. I'm not sure how I even got there, so I don't know that I could offer any useful advice at this point.

I wasn't there long enough to gain an in-depth view of the bigger challenges they might have to deal with, but because of the degree of cooperation between people and nature, it would be unlikely that an ocean would ever go rampaging across their landscape simply because it would immediately return to its basin when asked by the people. Even though I have not developed a clear practice of going there, or the guidelines for doing so, it is helpful to know that such a place exists and we could possibly go there if this Earth gets too messy.

As an alternative, we may also be able to enter a frequency range with a state of consciousness whose signature is different from the one we live with daily on Planet Earth, but similar enough that we hardly realize that we have shifted things. I have been out of the body many times and the realities I sometimes find myself in are often so similar to our everyday waking reality that I can barely tell the difference. In the case of the micronova, the difference sought would be that the disaster does not occur.

The next possibility to consider is that those who develop their consciousness to an extraordinary level may be able to generate a temporary field around themselves that leaves them untouched by the disaster. Those who have gone to conferences or workshops where they walked on fiery coals without getting burned have some experience with this.[104] There are reports of Hawaiian kahunas who could walk across hot lava without being hurt,[105] and Eastern masters who could walk on water or levitate.[106] This is not magic. In the case of firewalking, it is the ability of the individual to put frequencies into play between the skin and the hot coals that prevent being burned. In the case of walking on water or levitating, it is communication with the frequencies of water or air and requesting that they perform as solids to support you.

This same principle of working with the consciousness embedded in frequencies is also evident in plant spirit medicine. Those who have worked with this kind of medicine have experienced times when a specific plant was needed for healing, but that plant was not available. The healer will then ask another plant to step in and change its chemistry in order to get the job done. By giving the plant a short time to make the change (about 20 minutes) it can then be used to make the needed medicine. Plants are willing and able to step in and make whatever changes are necessary to help with healing. If they can do this, why can't we?

There is also the possibility of learning to draw in or internally generate the energies needed to supply the body with what it needs in terms of nutrition and keeping itself healthy without eating. I have gone for long periods with very little food. A friend of mine stopped eating about four years ago. He just woke up one day and thought, "I'm not going to eat." He didn't suffer headaches, didn't lose any weight, didn't get crabby or feel deprived. He's still not eating. Anything is possible when you can shift and develop your consciousness!

⚘

When we talk about responding to the effects of a micro-nova, we are talking about a response to an emergency that needs to be fully aware

---

104 Encyclopedia Brittanica, *Fire-walking Religious Ceremony;* https://www.britannica.com/topic/fire-walking.

105 Phillip Rasch, *Fire-Walking and the Huna Instances*, The Round Robin, Vol. 02, No. 06. https://borderlandsciences.org/journal/vol/02/n06/Rasch_on_Fire-Walking_Huna.html.

106 Spalding, Baird T. *Life and Teaching of the Masters of the Far East*, DeVorss Publications, Marina del Rey, CA. P. 52-55.

and automatic. You can't panic and collapse in overwhelm at the critical moment. When I first took classes in martial arts, the teacher had us do the same thing every week. We practiced a set of moves again and again. After a month, I was bored and complained that I wanted to do something new, something exciting. The next week the teacher came barreling through the group of students, pushing, shoving and attacking. Everyone reacted differently. Some tried to get out of the way, some folded immediately, some tried to fight back, and nobody used the set of kadas that we had been practicing, including me. In the discussion that followed, I began to understand that the goal was to respond to the critical moment automatically with the right moves and appropriate power. Developing consciousness is the same. You practice and practice until your response to an emergency, an accident, an attack, argument, or any other situation is automatic and uses the appropriate amount of power married to a commanding intent. The intent requires that you know what you want, and the power is the emotional punch behind that intent. When that response is always a form of real love, not the sappy stuff that passes for love in today's world, you will know you are getting there. Real love is an honest response.

By developing consciousness, we may be able to alter reality, alter events, or at least alter the impact of events we are subjected to. For example, those of us living in the U.S. have heard reports of atrocities going on in Iraq or Syria. We know they're happening, and this knowledge impacts us, but the atrocities are happening elsewhere, they are not happening to us directly. We go about our daily lives in relative peace. This is similar to creating a temporary field of protection as in fire-walking but is long-term and long-distance instead.

There are many stories out there that talk about a time long ago when *the gods* lived and walked on earth. They weren't gods in the way religions talk about *God*, they were highly developed humans who had unfolded their human potential to a high degree—the same thing we are being pushed to do. ॐ

21 ✑

Messages From the Past

AFTER MONTHS OF ARGUING WITH MYSELF ABOUT WHETHER OR NOT TO say anything more than what I already said in *Trump and The Sting*, or share the information about the micro-nova, I finally decided that some people would want to know. There were four factors that convinced me to speak up.

One was the I message received many years ago that there were "six billion people on the planet who came at this time because they knew that Christ consciousness was going to be taught, and that we would need that mass of consciousness in the near future." The second was the influence of my own personal experiences with the Robes in watching the planet roll about in space, and the three beings of light who took me to visit another, more beautiful Earth. The third was the amount of scientific information that came together from so many fields and that perfectly answered so many unanswered questions that had been dangling for a century. And the fourth was the information from ancient sources—the flood stories from around the world; the Hindu stories of solar fire in the Mahabharata; the Mayans and their stories of the Fifth Sun; the Greeks and their stories of Atlantis; Edgar Cayce's mention in a few of his readings about people who managed to get to high ground and then watched the waters rise, destroying civilization; the Egyptian story of Ra, the sun god, who decided to punish humankind; and other sources.

In his book, *Worlds in Collision*, Immanuel Velikovsky points out that many people knew about the recurring destruction of the world by water and fire. "One of the most terrifying events in the past of mankind was the conflagration of the world, accompanied by awful apparitions in the sky, quaking of the earth, vomiting of lava by thousands of volcanoes, melting of the ground, boiling of the sea, submersion of continents, a primeval chaos bombarded by flying hot stones, the roaring of the cleft earth, and the loud hissing of tornadoes of cinders...it becomes apparent that the knowledge, which was possibly alive in Egypt in the days when Solon and Pythagoras visited there, had already sunk into oblivion by the Ptolemaic age. Only some hazy tradition about a conflagration of the world was repeated, without knowing when or how it occurred."[107]

One of the stops on my recent travels was in Kentucky where I was given the gift of a small book, *The 8 Calendars of the Maya*, by Hunbatz Men. As I read it, I realized that the reason the Maya were so interested in calendars was because they were tracking the cycles of destruction that occurred regularly on our planet. Their story of the successive suns was a perfect window into the variable impacts of the micro-nova cycle.

"The second sun must have brought with it very strong winds... stronger than tornadoes...The third sun brought with it great deluges that submerged many places on Earth...the result was that humanity was virtually exterminated...The beginning of the fourth sun almost exterminated humankind by fire...the Maya lived in caves...this should not be confused with the Stone Age, during which time humans also lived in caves. If the Maya lived in caves, it was for no other reason than that it was difficult to survive on the surface of Earth. Indeed, it is possible that the Sun may have scorched a great part of Earth's surface or else there were many volcanic eruptions."[108]

---

107 Immanuel Velikovsky, *Worlds in Collision*, Paradigma Ltd. 2009. P. 297-298.

108 Men, Hunbatz. *The 8 Calendars of the Maya*. Bear & Company, Rochester VT, 2010. P. 106-108.

The descendants of the Mayan Indians of Mesoamerica say we are in the Fifth Sun. They warn that when the current sun ends, our civilization will end just as it has at least four previous times. They say that when the world of modern man collapses, those who don't know how to live on the land will die. It is difficult to ignore the similarities between the information handed down to us from so many sources, and the information about what happens during the sun's micro-nova as outlined by Doug Vogt, Chan Thomas, and Ben Davidson.

If the micro-nova used to be common knowledge among ancient humanity, the question we face today would be one of timing. Doug Vogt says that the timing is regular and that it occurs every 12,068 years. Velikovsky agrees that great destructions occur, but he says there are major and minor versions of these events and they occur more frequently than Vogt's twelve thousand years because the solar system is much more dynamic and changing than we generally think it is. He says there was a destruction in the second millenium before Christ, and another, lesser one in 700-800 BC which was serious enough to affect clocks and calendars as the year increased from 360 days to 365¼ days.

Although Vogt says the 12,068 years is up in 2046, we really have no way of knowing if this will prove to be accurate or not. Because of the dire Y2K predictions that the tech world would collapse on New Year's Day in 2000 due to computer programming errors in the dates, and then the predictions that the entire world was going to collapse on Dec. 21, 2012, I am very leery of predicting dates. In truth, we don't need to know exact dates for such things. We need to pay attention and be ready.

As I was reading through the accounts from ancient history about the impact of the dust, fires, and floods, the material was daunting. "In the *Kalevala*, the Finnish epos which 'dates back to an enormous antiquity,' the time when the sun and moon disappeared from the sky, and dreaded shadows covered it, is described in these words:

> Even birds grew sick and perished,
> men and maidens, faint and famished,
> perished in the cold and darkness,
> from the absence of the sunshine,
> from the absence of the moonlight

But the wise men of the Northland
could not know the dawn of morning,
for the moon shines not in season
nor appears the sun at midday,
from their stations in the sky-vault."[109]

Many of the ancient texts paint such a glum view of what happens in the micro-nova that I had to ask myself if I even wanted to survive such an event. What if the aftermath of the nova is too much trauma, pain, and suffering? The question, "Would I rather leave this life?" was something I could not avoid. I ended up having to face death. This is why the necessity of developing consciousness is so important. Says Vogt, "We have 12,068 years to evolve to the Secret of the Universe, or be destroyed."

We may not know when there will be another micro-nova, but we know that we all leave here sooner or later. Being ready to step out of the body and remain fully conscious, aware, and alert is as important as being ready to push back at wind, fire, and water with all the power of consciousness you can muster. The important thing is recognize what is going on and how to respond with dignity and power.

The sun has changed color and is already beginning to swell. The magnetic poles are moving quickly. The Feb. 1, 2028 date seen as chaotic with a "crashing solar system" in the recent ZigZag journey was corroborated by a very good seer in New York who gave the date of 2027 as the start of the nova. He did not know about the results of the ZigZag, and I did not say anything about my own intuition that said it would begin in late 2027 and unfold from there. Once I see a date or even just an event, I remain open and watch. I don't mind being wrong. Things can change, and often do. In this case, I would LOVE to be wrong.

Whether or not the micro-nova happens in our lifetime, we still have to deal with the grand solar minimum, which also results in drastic changes. Are we prepared for 30+ years of colder temperatures and the possibility of snow and freezing temperatures in the middle of summer? What will that do to our food supply? If we have to deal with civil wars or

---

109 From *The Kalevala*, Rune, 49, in *Worlds in Collision*, Immanuel Velikovsky, Paradigma Ltd., 2009. P. 140.

trade wars, what should be set up and in place to make sure we can supply our needs? Amazon, Facebook, Google, and others are in the Trump crosshairs. Amazon has put many local retail stores out of business. Who will sell us what we need if Amazon goes away or comes apart?

It is entirely possible to avoid civil war in the U.S. even though we are not doing very well at avoiding the chaos created by attempts to divide us in many ways. The possibility of a break-up without a civil war would be unusual, but not impossible. How much responsibility are we willing to take for our governing system, which is really all about relationships?

∽

Not long after Q Anon began dropping information, he indicated they had video, audio, and photos documenting the criminal activities of politicians at the top who engaged in high treason, fraud, money laundering, sex trafficking, organ trafficking, drug trafficking, pedophilia, and child sacrifice. I was shocked. These are not the kinds of relationships that make an elegant, loving world. When he hinted that these photos, videos, and audios would be released to the public, I began to freak out a little. I have an extraordinary ability to process unusual or difficult information quickly and see the way forward, but I was disturbed for months after seeing those photos. I was haunted for weeks when my clairaudience tapped into some of the sounds at a child sacrifice ritual. The release of these videos, audios, and photos is liable to push us over the edge into full-blown unrest.

I do not know if we will be able to save our country. I do know we cannot go backwards to the good old days. We can only move ahead and use our entire experience to create new perceptions, new ideas, new pathways, inventions, and lifestyles that implement the hard-earned wisdom of the past and the dynamic promise of the future.

We Americans had to learn to kiss the Trump frog so that our future could be transformed. We have kissed the frog, showing that we are willing to do what is difficult, but we have not yet done the actual work. The frog is the consciousness of the future. The transformation of consciousness will allow us to shape that future and then step into it.

When consciousness changes, we will learn to see past the façades and illusions that are familiar and comfortable. Just because something is familiar and comfortable does not mean that anything good, ethical, or nurturing is happening. Many people are quite comfortable with deep dysfunction in their family or place of work. It is only by getting out of the box and choosing something different that we have a chance to become our full, powerful selves. If we do not allow ourselves to see beyond the illusions, then someone or something will force us to do so, and that is the challenge hanging over us.

Wars, economic collapse, conquest, and natural disasters are not the only ways a civilization can come to an end. It can also be transcended. To transcend anything successfully, we must take the basic organizing principles with us, but learn to apply them in new ways. The organizing principles of a successful civilization include: personal responsibility, collective cooperation, a humane form of self-governance, wise use of resources, social wisdom traditions, the celebration of culture as a set of survival tools, and a collective gratitude that there are others to share the journey with us.

We need new designs for relationships, governance, finance, business, for educating and healing ourselves, not to mention a totally new understanding of our history, our solar system, ourselves, and our great potential. We need to embrace lifelong learning as well as the centuries-long evolution of consciousness taking place at both the individual level *and* the level of our collective civilization.

The real goal while you are alive here is to wake up, expand consciousness, develop your power, and evolve yourself past death. In other words, we come to this reality system to learn how to sustain ourselves forever, to become eternal beings. It appears we may be about to have our first real test.

Planet Earth is a powerful consciousness generator and a great place for beginners wishing to reach immortality. It is only here, in a physical realm that there is enough stability to practice stabilizing yourself as an eternal being. Other reality systems are not as stable and do not make the best setting for beginners who are learning the critical skills of consciousness. In the classic Trickster setup, it is *consciousness* that has to change. If Q Anon releases his last tranche of photos, audio, and video information, we could have a full-blown crisis of consciousness on top of civil war *and* a crashing solar system.

&

As mentioned earlier, sometimes it takes a long time to figure out how to put the pieces of your life together in a way that makes sense, a way that allows you to draw the most wisdom, power, and grace from them. In *Consciousness and Energy, Vol. 3*, I had an epiphany when I realized that the elves on my farm were pushing me to enter into a full, communicating relationship with Nature. I thought I knew why.

Now I look at the elves' communications with me, and see that they were coaxing me back into that relationship with Nature for reasons other than the ones I first assumed. The way they went about it demonstrated their love of fun, interesting experience, joyful creation, and deep purpose. They didn't start with, "Hey, you need to get involved with Nature because there's a disaster coming!" They started in plenty of time so that they could teach me gently and with lots of humor at first, gradually pulling me toward the more serious aspects of what they wanted, which was for us to begin communicating with the elements, and stretch consciousness to survive. They made it clear that we had to reconnect with Mother Nature.

The Robes said the same thing—that if we did not reconnect with Mother Nature, we would not survive. I thought I knew what they meant, too, but now I see a much deeper message. The message is, if you don't develop your consciousness to re-establish the relationship with all of Nature, you will be overwhelmed by the coming changes in your country, your government, the sun, the Earth, and the weather elements of wind, rain, heat, snow, ice, and soil. The elements are the ones that are most easily communicated with because we deal with them every day in the form of the weather.

If we are going to survive the sun's nova cycle, the key piece we need right now is the ability to communicate with the elements. What if we could keep the majority of the ocean calm and in its basin, or at least direct it to the places of least damage? What if we could quiet the wind or strengthen the buildings? What if we could stabilize the earth and calm the animals? What if we could make things much easier for ourselves? On the other hand, what if we could step into life on another Earth and live there quite well? Do we want to survive such a massive natural disaster? What would we face in the aftermath? What do we face if we leave here?

Even if we choose not to survive here, the need to develop consciousness is still critical. One of my students complained saying, if this is what we have to look forward to, what is the point of developing consciousness and why are we wasting time here in this life?

The idea of wasting time is only valid in a material world where we have been programmed to let go of our natural inclination to cooperate with all things. Instead we engage in competitive behaviors that we think will bring us money, material goods, worldly power, and status. The development of consciousness calls us to be present in ourselves every minute right up to the very last moment of physical life, at which time we then step quietly into the next world, intact and coherent, aware, powerful, and ready to help others who may be struggling with the transition. Being present to what is happening can help us to move immediately to the next world without trauma or missing a beat.

We have all had dreams from which we waken instantly the moment something frightening or overwhelming occurs. We tell ourselves it was just a dream. But a dream is not just a dream. It is a real experience that we are creating in another reality system and from which we can withdraw suddenly to protect the ability of consciousness to adapt without trauma. While we are in that other reality system, our life back here in this system is viewed as a dream. *It's all a dream.* And because it's all a dream, we can waken from anything too overwhelming. We can move into a lucid state at any moment, and when we do, the rules change, the possibilities change, and the outcomes change, sometimes dramatically, sometimes to something that looks and feels quite normal. Developing consciousness is central to all of these. Leaving consciousness in the box and trying to ignore the future is probably not the best decision.

Let's move ahead…gently, fiercely, full of consciousness. ✥

Index

Symbols

A

B

Penny Kelly, N.D. is a writer, teacher, international consultant, speaker, publisher, and Naturopathic physician. She is the owner of Lily Hill Farm and Learning Center in southwest Michigan where she teaches courses in *Developing the Gift of Intuition, Getting Well Again Naturally,* and *Organic Gardening.* Penny has been researching consciousness, cognition, perception, and intelligence for over 35 years. She has written seven books of her own, as well as co-written 23 books with others. She is the mother of four children and lives in Lawton, MI where she raises organic vegetables, chickens, and cows.

Her website is www.consciousnessonfire.com

Other Books by Penny Kelly:

The Evolving Human – A True Story of Awakened Kundalini

The Elves of Lily Hill Farm

Robes – A Book of Coming Changes

Getting Well Again, Naturally

Consciousness and Energy, Vol. 1 – Multi-dimensionality and a Theory of Consciousness

Consciousness and Energy, Vol. 2 – New Worlds of Energy

Consciousness and Energy, Vol. 3 – Religion, Sex, Power, and the Fall of Consciousness

Child of the Brown Earth – small book of poems

CPSIA information can be obtained
at www.ICGtesting.com
Printed in the USA
BVHW071644120720
583397BV00001B/63